YORKSHIRE TERRIER

EDITED BY
BRENDA PIPES

ACKNOWLEDGEMENTS

The publishers would like to thank the following for help with photography: Wendy White Thomas (Wenwytes); Janet Redhead (Jankeri); Rita Harbury (Antara); Kay Morris (Wedgewood) and Suzanne Robertsson (Doggy-Boons); Amanda Bulbeck; Hearing Dogs for Deaf People; Pets As Therapy.

Cover photo: © Tracy Morgan Animal Photography (www.animalphotographer.co.uk)
Dog featured is Frasermar Tempting Kisses JW, owned by Mr. Stuart
Thomas Carruthers, bred by Margaret Conrie-Bryant.

Page 2 © istockphoto.com/Pavel Timofeyev; Page 8 © istockphoto.com/Lisa Thornberg;
Page 12 © istockphoto.com/Katherine Moffitt; Page 15 © istockphoto.com/Ben Lynn;
Page 20 (top) © istockphoto.com/Francisco Orellana; Page 20 (bottom) © istockphoto.com/Andrey Medvedev;
Page 39 © istockphoto.com/Joey Nelson; Page 41 © istockphoto.com/Nataliya Kuznetsova;
Page 57 © istockphoto.com/Donna Coleman; Page 58 © istockphoto.com/Vladimir Suponev;
Page 63 © istockphoto.com/photopix; Page 69 © istockphoto.com/Natalia Sdobnikova;
Page 72 © istockphoto.com/Alexandr Ryzhov; Page 82 © istockphoto.com/G Prentice;
Page 87 © istockphoto.com/Pavel Timofeyev; Page 107 © istockphoto.com/cynoclub;
Page 122 © istockphoto.com/Konstantin Gushcha; Pages 123 and 142 © istockphoto.com/Wojciech Pusz

The British Breed Standard reproduced in Chapter 7 is the copyright of the Kennel Club and published with the club's kind permission. Extracts from the American Breed Standard are reproduced by kind permission of the American Kennel Club.

THE QUESTION OF GENDER
The 'he' pronoun is used throughout this book instead of the rather impersonal 'it', but no gender bias is intended

First published in 2011 by The Pet Book Publishing Company Limited
PO Box 8, Lydney, Gloucestershire GL15 6YD

ISBN
978-1-906305-43-7
1-906305-43-9

Printed and bound in China by PWGS

CONTENTS

GETTING TO KNOW YORKSHIRE TERRIERS

Chapter 1

The popular Yorkshire Terrier is one of the smallest dogs around, yet his diminutive stature belies a bold, inquisitive nature – this is a large dog in a small body.

The Yorkshire Terrier is man-made from a variety of other breeds, going back more than 150 years. During the Industrial Revolution many people moved around the country, seeking work. Among them were workers from the far north of Scotland and their dogs, which may have included the Clydesdale, Paisley, Skye and Waterside Terriers. Some of the workers settled in the north of England (Leeds, Manchester and Huddersfield), where their dogs were mixed with the Black and Tan or Manchester Terrier and other broken-haired breeds to develop into what, in the mid 1800s, were frequently referred to as

Broken Haired Scotch Terriers, and eventually became known as Yorkshire Terriers. The Kennel Club recognised the breed as a Yorkshire Terrier in a stud book in 1874.

At that stage the breed was a lot bigger than today and was used for sport, i.e. ratting in the pits for wagers. The first successful dog was Huddersfield Ben who, it was claimed, killed 100 rats in 30 seconds. However, the Yorkie's loyal and fun-loving nature also attracted a following of dog lovers. As the breed became more popular and breeding became more standardised, the Yorkshire Terrier has more than halved in size. Originally weighing more than 15 lbs (7 kgs), the ideal weight for today's Yorkie is no more than 7 lbs (3.2 kgs). *For further detail, see Chapter Two: The First Yorkshire Terriers.*

PHYSICAL CHARACTERISTICS

The Yorkshire Terrier's small size and tough, outgoing personality is a surprise to most people who get to know this charming dog. The breed has become a family favourite companion and guard-dog rolled into one. This small dynamic dog has a way of dominating an owner or becoming his best friend. His smart terrier head is usually held high when out walking. He is always alert and, more often than not, his ears are erect, looking out to meet and greet people.

COAT TYPES

Depending on whether a Yorkie is in show coat or has a pet trim, he can look quite different, although both types have a coat of silky steel-blue on the back with a rich tan chest. Most pet Yorkies have the coat clipped to a manageable length, which needs doing about two or three times a year. Show dogs require a great deal more work.

Growing a full coat can take the best part of two years, attending to the coat from about 10 weeks of age with daily grooming and weekly bathing. But remember, this is the dog's crowning glory and is only needed if you are going to show him. It is much easier for you and the dog to have him pet-trimmed. In all aspects a pet Yorkie is as good as a show Yorkie.

COLOUR AND TEXTURE

The Yorkie coat can come in many colours of blue and also many textures. The show coat should be dark steel-blue – spoken of long ago as the colour of a split piece of coal, dark and shiny, and the texture of silk. If you have a silk scarf and you hold it between your fingers, it slips through your fingers and feels cold to touch, just as a show coat should. Over the years we have refined our breeding practices to develop the right colour and texture, but it has taken time and research. Because of this, many people try the quick-fix treatment of colouring the coat. This has been going on for many years, but all over the world this practice is against kennel club rules. If caught the exhibitor will be fined

and possibly banned from showing in the UK. Because this goes on at the highest level, what you see isn't always what you get. I should point out that this practice is not exclusive to Yorkshire Terrier exhibitors – it happens in all breeds, large and small.

If you do intend to show, do your homework and choose the best dog you can afford from established lines that have been proven in the show ring so that you know the colour is real and correct. Do not cheat, as the only person you are fooling is yourself. If your dog's coat is slightly lighter than others, then you know it is an honest colour. It is

A Yorkshire Terrier in full glory with a coat that touches the ground.

better to advance slowly and get there than to cheat and be found out later.

DOCKING

Docking has not been allowed in the UK since the Animal Welfare Act came into force in 2007 although it is still permitted in the US. It is also banned in Europe and Scandinavia. You cannot import a docked dog and show him. Certain working breeds can be docked but it must be by a vet and the correct paperwork and microchipping must also be given to prove that it is legal.

Dogs docked before 2007 may still be shown in the ring. Before the practice became illegal we arranged for the vet to dock our dogs at about two to three days of age, before the cartilage had started to develop. Within a few moments pup was back with mum. We docked at a slightly shorter length than is currently seen in the US.

LONGEVITY

On the whole, this little terrier has an amazing life span, living well into his teens. It has even been known for a Yorkshire Terrier to make it to 20 years. However, this is exceptional; most Yorkies will be with you until about 12 years old, some until they are 16.

The other side of the coin is the unexplained death at a much younger age of seven or eight years. It just seems to be a landmark and it is not understood why this is sometimes the case.

Most pet owners opt for a trim that is easy to maintain.

YORKIES AND ALLERGIES

The Yorkshire Terrier has a coat that is ideal for people with allergies. The single, silky-textured coat, if looked after properly, collects little dust and can be bathed regularly.

The Yorkshire Terrier is classified as a Toy dog – but he is a real terrier at heart.

Always bear in mind that however much time you have with your Yorkie, you should enjoy it to the full.

A REAL DOG

The Yorkie is classified in the Toy Group in the UK, but in Europe he is in the Terrier Group. This spirited little dog has a typical terrier nature. This being so, you must remember that he is a dog and not a toy. While a Yorkie can be fiercely loyal and affectionate, like all terrier breeds (indeed, like dogs of all breeds) he can quickly become bored and destructive without sufficient stimulation (physical and mental) and good leadership,

TEMPERAMENT

The importance of breeding and socialisation cannot be underestimated, but, even so, every Yorkie is unique. That said, there are some traits that are characteristic of the breed as a whole. For example, the Yorkie is nosy, often checking out every little nook and cranny, and bringing you presents that you have just planted in the garden. He is quick to learn and enthusiastic. Playing fetch is one of the first time-consuming games you are likely to be faced with from your new pet.

Brave and loyal, once your Yorkie is settled in his new home, it is likely that any unexpected noise will be met with barking. Always willing to please, this is a breed that, given the time to train, will do well at obedience or mini-agility. Although he can be very active, do not think that a Yorkie likes to be busy all the time; he likes nothing better than snuggling up with someone on the sofa for an hour or two.

Like all breeds, the Yorkshire Terrier is not an angel. He can get up to mischief when left to amuse himself for too long. The golden rule is: if you have to leave your dog for any amount of time, invest in a puppy-pen or large crate.

TRAINABILITY

The best way to ensure your Yorkie behaves as an ideal pet is to provide adequate stimulation with regular exercise and training. Some canine activities combine elements of both, such as agility (see Chapter 6). Basic training, involving obedience commands, is also a good way of reinforcing your leadership status. Training a Yorkie is as easy or as hard as you want to make it. Anything learned with an element of fun makes the job easier. If you don't enjoy training then neither will your dog.

A Yorkie loves tidbits, so it's always good to keep a number of treats with you as a reward. Be positive during training, and, when giving commands, remember that short words have more impact than a string of conversation. Most dogs want to please, but if you are rambling on when you are trying to discipline him, the message gets confused and often you encourage the wrong behaviour. Praise a good dog. Ignore a bad one. If this is done when the pup is very new then this is a good start for owner and dog alike.

Joining a club will help prevent you from making any training mistakes, as well as encouraging you to train regularly. It is also a good means of continuing socialisation around other dogs and people. As a follow-on from this, you could enrol your Yorkie on the Kennel Club Good Citizen Scheme (see Chapter 6). This teaches owners and dogs how to behave in all sorts of situations.

When you are training your dog, remember that commands must be precise and direct. Do not over-complicate what you want your dog to do. In the wrong hands, the intelligent Yorkie can be a master of manipulation. For example, if your dog dances about and runs away from you, turn your back on him and walk away. Do not chase him, as you are handing him control. Games should be played on your terms; you are the one who should start the game and end it. If bad habits start – eating stones, peeing in the wrong place – it may be a form of attention-seeking, or maybe you have given the wrong signals when this started. Chattering to a dog when there is bad behaviour encourages him to do it again. Ignore a dog when he is trying to get your attention for the wrong reasons and praise good behaviour. You cannot explain to a dog why he has done something wrong; all he understands is that he has your attention and so he will do it again to get the same response. If

YORKIES AND CELEBRITIES

Yorkies are a popular dog and are quite a fashion statement among celebrities. But you don't have to be Sharon Osbourne, Victoria Beckham or Joan Collins to get a lot of fun out of your dog. Unfortunately, when the media features a dog as a fashion item it is the breed that suffers. Money can and does buy you anything. Hopefully you will want a Yorkie for his character and not because a celeb has got one.

you find that you have made these errors and cannot find a way to undo it, there are canine behaviourists that are willing to give you and your dog the necessary guidance.

THINGS TO CONSIDER

Before you acquire a Yorkshire Terrier, there are a few important points to consider. Dog ownership (of any breed) means taking on a lot of responsibility and adjusting your life to accommodate an animal that will look to you for all his needs.

COUNTING THE COST

Although generally healthy, the Yorkie will require you to set aside some money for his care. If you are buying your Yorkie from a breeder, you may have to pay a

large amount of money. However, even rescue centres tend to ask for a donation of some sort to cover their costs, so this should be factored into your plans. You will also have to buy various pieces of equipment for your pet, such as a dog bed, collar and lead, crate/pen, feeding bowls, grooming equipment, etc. Then there will be the expense of having your dog vaccinated and possibly microchipped. Of course, your dog is worth it, but it is prudent to work out how you plan to pay for all this well in advance of getting your pet.

In addition to the initial outlay, you will have to cover ongoing expenses, such as buying food and covering the costs of routine care, such as worming tablets, flea/tick treatments, and possible visits to a dog groomer.

Always remember that, like all dogs, Yorkies occasionally need emergency veterinary care, so keep a 'piggy bank' for these times. It is always worth having your pup insured, at least for the first few years, as this is the time when youngsters have their crazy moments and get bumps and knocks that need attention. Broken bones can be caused by the silliest moments or just forgetting that this little dog

usually follows you like a shadow until he feels confident enough to be exploring by himself. Do not leave him on the sofa while you go and make a cup of tea, for example, as, if he falls, that could be the end of any long walks.

EXERCISE
Small he may be, but the Yorkshire Terrier has a lot of energy. He is a good little mover and can walk many miles. He is a favourite with hill walkers as a

companion. The rugged little Yorkie can manage the most uneven ground, and when he does run out of steam, he is small enough to go in a rucksack for a rest. Agility is another favourite pastime for the Yorkie.

If you are active and have the energy, a Yorkie may be the breed for you. There are some inherited physical problems associated with the breed, such as luxating patella (slipping kneecap), but if you choose your breeder

In most cases, a Yorkie will enjoy the company of older children and adults.

carefully, you should end up with a healthy dog that has no problems.

After a particularly active day, the Yorkshire Terrier loves to come home and be a couch potato (as long as there is company to do this with), and this makes his small size another advantage, of course.

For more details on exercise, see Chapter Three: A Yorkie for your Lifestyle.

CHILDREN AND YORKIES

A Yorkshire Terrier can be a child's best friend if mutual respect is established. From about four years of age, a small child can prove to be a never-ending food supply for this little terrier. But remember that human food, especially chocolate, is extremely bad for dogs and keeping your Yorkie fit means no treats except when training your dog. It is also vital that the child respects the dog and understands that he is not a toy that can be pulled around. A young puppy will also need plenty of rest through the day. An indoor crate or an exercise pen is ideal for giving your Yorkie some quiet 'down time'.

Children younger than four years old are not really suitable companions for this fast little dog. The problem is that a toddler is still struggling to understand what 'no' means, and it is all too easy for problems to occur. The older the child, the more responsibility he or she can be given to look after a dog. This encourages a better understanding on both sides. For the future, the chance of showing in junior handling or obedience would be great fun for both. It is lovely to see proud parents watching their children in classes at shows.

OLD FRIENDS

Selling a dog to an elderly couple or an older person can be a wonderful experience. The new 'baby' will be loved and cosseted, and he will provide motivation for those who need something to get up for in the morning. He is easy to look after and will not demand too much exercise, as long as mental stimulation is provided. However, before taking on a Yorkie, the question should be asked: 'Have provisions been made in case of illness or death? Not surprisingly, older people are more than one step ahead and, in every case, I have found that arrangements have been put in place.

Remember, the breeder is there to help you. If you cannot find someone to take on your Yorkie if your situation changes, it may be that the dog can be bequeathed back to the breeder to be looked after or rehomed. I would certainly not prevent an elderly person from taking on a Yorkie.

The adaptable Yorkie will fit in with a variety of different lifestyles.

out-walk a Labrador or Pointer. I recall someone having a larger Yorkie with two Rottweilers, and the Yorkie was the boss of all he surveyed. He always made sure he was the one with the big bed while the Rotties had to make do with the cold floor.

As with all interactions, good socialisation and careful introductions are the key to successful mixing.

HOLIDAYS & TRAVEL

It is a great bonus if you can take your Yorkie on holiday with you. Being small enough to fit in a carry box, most hotels will accept a dog that is well looked after and obedient. It is quite fashionable these days to holiday with your dog and many hotels and cottages do now oblige.

If you are going on holiday or transporting your Yorkie anywhere for any reason, it is important that you ensure he travels safely. Fashions come and go and all sorts of bags and carriers are available for transporting small Toy dogs. However, a crate or carry box is sturdier, has a flat bottom to stand on, and probably costs half the price. If all else fails, the front passenger-side footwell is the safest place for your dog to travel if he is unrestrained.

It is now possible to take your dog abroad on holiday to certain countries without lengthy quarantine periods. This requires various health checks, plus vaccination against rabies, which your veterinary surgeon would be able to discuss with you.

Yorkshire Terriers can mix well with bigger breeds – as long as initial interactions are supervised.

YORKIES AND OTHER PETS

Yorkies enjoy company – be it on four legs or two. There is nothing funnier than to see a Yorkie playing chase with a couple of kittens. Mixing big and small only works if the temperaments of both animals are trustworthy and you have a confident owner who understands their dogs. The Yorkie by nature is a ratter and it would be very unwise for an owner to leave rabbits, birds, or any other small pet unattended with this little stalker.

MORE THAN ONE?

Two or three Yorkshire Terriers are great together, as they keep themselves amused and cause laughter with their antics. You will find that they always eat better when there is more than one (this is about the only breed that does not automatically clean the dish down to the pattern each and every meal time).

It is quite surprising that, often, the more unequal the mix, the more often it works. Little and large! Yorkies can often

Holidays will be even more fun if you can take your Yorkie with you.

If you unable to take your Yorkshire Terrier on holiday, there may be suitable boarding kennels that would be willing to take your pet. These need to be vetted to get an idea of the facilities – if you can contact other people who have used them or can recommend them, so much the better. Never leave a Yorkshire Terrier in a kennel unless you feel happy with their care, as not all kennels cater for small dogs. Yorkshire Terriers really do like their home comforts.

Home boarding is another option whereby a recommended person house-sits while you are away and can look after your pet, house and plants as desired. If possible, recruit a family member to do this job, as your pet will know the person and is more likely to be better behaved and more settled.

THE IDEAL HOME

The ideal home for a Yorkshire Terrier is with someone who will spend large amounts of time at home with the dog. Given plenty of time and attention, a typical Yorkie will adapt well to most living arrangements.

The ideal home for a Yorkshire Terrier can be a little terraced house with a backyard or a mansion with acres to run in. A flat or apartment is probably the least desirable situation for this small, active dog. But I have known owners who do not have the luxury of a garden but have coped very well with a litter tray for 'urgent use' and field and forest for busy days out, be it in rain, hail or sun. Always remember that a happy dog comes from a happy home.

THE RIGHT PUPPY

Your Yorkshire Terrier's temperament will be influenced greatly by his breeding and early socialisation. Breeding with well-tempered stock is essential, as any animal who has not had the best start is susceptible to uncertain behaviour. A puppy will be influenced by his genetic make-up – the temperament of his sire and dam, and other close relatives in his bloodlines – and also by his environment. A puppy reared in a threatening environment (several boisterous children, for example) is unlikely to do well. The golden rule is to find the right pup for the right owner. Sometimes it is better to walk away from a puppy that you feel is not the one than to be talked into taking him. A good breeder will take the time to find out about your home life and match you with the right puppy, and would prefer you to say no if the match is not right.

YORKSHIRE TERRIER

ASSISTANCE DOGS

The Yorkshire Terrier has proven his ability as an assistance dog.
Top left: Hearing Dog Bertie – winner of the 2003 Golden Bonio Award for saving the life of a hospital patient by alerting staff that the patient had stopped breathing.
Bottom left: Hearing Dog Jodie.
Above: Therapy Dog Benny.

ESTABLISHING A ROUTINE

Dogs like routine and it is best to set one from the first day. Everyone in the family – dogs, children and adults – should have clear rules to follow, and, hopefully, within a week or two, life will adjust to a set pattern. It is often best to get the new pup home by mid afternoon; to give him time to familiarise himself with your home and family. The Yorkie adjusts well to a routine put in place by someone who has established themselves as a pack leader (see Chapter 6).

ADAPTABILITY

The Yorkshire Terrier makes an excellent PAT (Pets as Therapy) dog, as he loves attention.

These little terriers make good warning dogs, and, with specialised training, they can also become hearing dogs. The UK charity Hearing Dogs for Deaf People has several Yorkshire Terriers on its books. One of the main advantages of using this breed is that their small size allows them to adapt to living even in a small flat (as long as adequate exercise is given).

SUMMARY

With his intelligence, adaptability, and eager-to-please personality, the Yorkshire Terrier is equally at home in a one-to-one environment or as part of a larger group. He is not a solitary creature, however, and will become depressed if he is left on his own for long periods. Given plenty of company, stimulation and exercise, he will make a much-loved addition to any home and prove himself to be a totally devoted companion.

THERAPY DOGS

It is well established that dogs can have tremendous therapeutic benefits, and there are now many charities worldwide that promote the services of therapy dogs. These dogs, who are carefully selected, visit people in hospitals, hospices, care homes, day care centres, special needs schools and many other establishments, as well as working with children who suffer from animal phobias, helping them to live a normal life in the community. Maureen Hennis, Chief Executive of Pets As Therapy (P.A.T.) in the UK says:

PAT Chief Executive Maureen Hennis.

"There is no doubt about it, dogs are a very important part of our lives. They cheer us and give comfort when we are depressed, keep us healthy and active, make us laugh and generally improve our quality of life. Therefore the pain of being denied access to animals can be unbearable."

For more than 17 years Maureen visited a nursing home with two of her own registered P.A.T. dogs, Dippy and Harriet, both Yorkshire Terriers. She remembers one patient used to sit by the door waiting for the visit from the P.A.T. dogs. Each week her cry would be the same "Here's my ray of sunshine, she's my reason for staying alive". A tiny Yorkshire Terrier evoked this wonderful reaction.

Maureen has also worked closely with people who suffer from phobias, and she vividly recalls one young boy who used to be literally frozen with fear around dogs. With considerable perseverance, and the help of several P.A.T. dogs including one of Maureen's Yorkies this boy overcame his fear and actually came to look forward to meeting dogs.

Although Maureen no longer visits with her own dogs, largely due to her position as Chief Executive of Pets As Therapy, she is in no doubt about the value Yorkshire Terriers can have in this role. She says "their small size make them ideal as P.A.T. dogs, because they are small enough to be easily cuddled and stroked by an elderly, possibly frail person. Their size also makes them among the least threatening of dogs – ideal for someone who is nervous around dogs or who may have a phobia. And their fun loving, affectionate personality means they really do bring a ray of sunshine into the lives of people they meet."

Maureen's beloved Yorkie Harriet, who brightened the lives of many.

THE FIRST YORKSHIRE TERRIERS

Chapter 2

The origins of the Yorkshire Terrier are not recorded in any books discovered to date, but their ancestors were most certainly working dogs mainly kept to keep down vermin such as rats. It is accepted that the roots of the Yorkshire Terrier lie in Scotland. Dogs were brought down to Yorkshire during the industrial revolution in the 19th century when many Scots travelled to the Yorkshire Ridings, seeking work in the mines and mills. It is said that the weavers used to stroke the dogs that were used for keeping the rat populations down in the weaving sheds, and the lanolin on their hands protected and conditioned the dogs' coats and made them shine.

Originally the Yorkshire Terrier was known as a rough or Broken-haired Scotch Terrier. It was much heavier than the little dogs we know today, weighing more than 15 lbs (7-8 kgs)), where today the Breed Standard asks for dogs under 7 lbs (3.2 kgs).

TERRIER BREEDS

It is thought that a number of breeds contributed to the make-up of the Yorkshire Terrier, among them the Skye Terrier, the Clydesdale Terrier and the Paisley Terrier, and perhaps the English Black and Tan Toy Terrier and the Maltese Terrier, too. The Skye and Clydesdale Terriers were large dogs, weighing about 18 lbs (8 kgs), while the Paisley Terrier was a little smaller, weighing in at about 12 lbs (5.4 kgs). When bred with the tiny Maltese and Black and Tan Terriers, which weighed only about 4-6 lbs (1.8-2.7 kgs), the resulting offspring was much smaller, more refined and elegant.

SYKE TERRIER

The Skye Terrier takes its name from the Island of Skye, one of the Inner Hebrides off the north-west coast of Scotland. The breed is thought to be one of the oldest Scottish Terrier breeds. It was primarily used for controlling vermin although, like many other breeds, it also gained popularity in the show world and as a pet. One of the most famous Skye Terriers of all was Greyfriars Bobby, working companion to policeman John Gray. This little terrier achieved fame for the 14-year vigil he kept at his erstwhile master's grave.

CLYDESDALE TERRIER

The Clydesdale Terrier hails from the Clyde Valley in Scotland – from which the breed takes its name. The Clydesdale was used largely for vermin control, although they were also kept as pets and exhibited in the show

Greyfriar's Bobby's exceptional loyalty is celebrated with a statue in Edinburgh.

The Skye Terrier was hugely influential in the development of the Yorkshire Terrier.

The Maltese may have been bred with the Black and Tan Terrier to provide a long coat.

ring, mainly in the area around Glasgow. The height of the breed's popularity was in the late 1870s. By the turn of the century its popularity in the show ring had waned, and, by the outbreak of the First World War, it had become extinct.

Accounts of the Clydesdale Terrier describe it as being a soft-coated Skye Terrier, in a colour of bright steel blue, with the head, legs and feet a clear golden tan, free from grey, sooty or black hairs. The colours described here are very similar to the Yorkshire Terrier we know today – the adjective 'sooty' is still in the Breed Standard. The parting of the coat extended from the head to the tail, hanging evenly down each side. I believe this breed may have had the biggest influence on the Yorkshire Terrier, but no one knows for certain.

PAISLEY TERRIER

The Paisley Terrier was very similar to the Clydesdale. Originating from Paisley in the Glasgow area, this breed was kept mainly in the weaving sheds, to keep the vermin population down. They were also kept as house pets. The head had a fairly long skull, and was flat and very narrow between the ears. It gradually widened towards the eyes and tapered very slightly to the nose, which was always black. The jaws were strong and the teeth were level (meaning the front of the upper and lower jaws meet exactly). The ears were small, set very high on the top of the head, and carried perfectly

A Yorkshire Terier pictured about 1880

erect. They were covered with long, silky hair hanging down by the sides of the head. The eyes were medium in size, dark in colour, not prominent, but having a sharp terrier-like expression. The eyelids were black.

The Paisley Terrier's body was long, deep in the chest, and well ribbed up. The back was perfectly level. The legs were as short and straight as possible, well set under the body, and entirely covered with silky hair. The feet were round and cat-like; the tail was perfectly straight, carried almost level with the back, and heavily feathered. The colour could be various shades of blue – dark blue for preference. The hair on the head and lower extremities was slightly lighter than the body above, but not a linty (fawn) shade. The coat had to be as long and straight as possible, free from all traces of curl or waviness, very glossy and silky in texture, with an entire absence of undercoat. The general appearance was of a long, low, level dog, with heavily fringed erect ears, and a long coat like the finest silk, or spun glass, which hung quite straight and evenly down each side from a parting extending from the nose to the root of the tail.

BLACK AND TAN TERRIER

The miniature Black and Tan Terrier was used for poaching rabbits. A dog would be sent down a rabbit hole to bolt the prey into the net, which was spread over the exit. The dog and rabbits were then put into the poacher's large pockets for a hasty retreat. The miniature Black and Tan had a smooth, silky coat, so was a little difficult to pull out of a rabbit hole. It was the canny Yorkshireman, looking for a more commercial breed, who bred these little dogs with a long-coated breed – possibly a Maltese Terrier – to enable the poachers to pull the dog out by his hair for a quick getaway.

TERRIER MIX

Possibly all the breeds mentioned above went into the make-up of the Yorkshire Terrier. Eventually, a distinct new type of dog would have emerged, possibly with different characteristics dependent on which breeder planned the mating. Further breeding of these different types would have eventually stabilised the emerging new breed, and, as certain features became more and more desirable, a lot of money would have changed hands for a dog of particular

FATHER OF THE BREED

The father of the breed was born in 1865. He was called Huddersfield Ben and his Kennel Club studbook number was 3612. By today's Standard, he was a fairly large dog, as he was shown in classes over 7 lbs (3.2 kgs) but under 12 lbs (5.2 kgs). He was bred by Mr W. Eastwood and was bought and shown successfully by Mrs Jonas Foster (Mary Ann), of Lister Hills, Bradford. This lady played a very important role in promoting the Yorkshire Terrier in its early days. Mrs Foster started out as a weaver and eventually married the owner of the mill, Jonas Foster. She was the first lady to judge the Yorkshire Terrier worldwide.

Unfortunately, Huddersfield Ben died at the early age of six years. Despite this, however, he was sire to many beautiful dogs, thus helping to shape this early breed. His offspring were regularly shown in classes under 7 lbs (3.2 kgs) or even under 5 lbs (2.2 kgs), so it would seem that Huddersfield Ben was a very consistent sire.

breeding, especially the very small dogs. Over time this would have resulted in the typical Yorkshire Terrier we think of today.

NAMING THE BREED
By the 1850s dogs were being exhibited at shows, although in those days the shows were mainly held in public houses. Initially, the Yorkshire Terrier was classed as a Scotch Terrier; it wasn't until the 1870s that this little dog became known as the Yorkshire Terrier, probably because the breed had been much improved in Yorkshire.

There were very good examples being bred in the north of England, where the development of a long, silky coat transformed him from a working dog to a beautiful, much-admired show dog.

The English Kennel Club was founded in 1873, after which time importance was placed on parentage. Pedigrees were documented. Knowing the typical characteristics of the dogs that featured prominently in the ancestry of successful show dogs allowed for a Yorkshire Terrier Breed Standard to be drawn up, setting down

some of these desirable characteristics in print. The Kennel Club recognised the breed as a Yorkshire Terrier in a stud book in 1874.

THE FIRST CHAMPIONS
The first Champion, I believe, was Abraham Bolton's Ch. Bright. His father was the famous Huddersfield Ben. The second Champion was Ms M.A. Troughear's Ch. Conqueror, who was later exported to America. The third champion, and the first champion bitch, was Mr Rhodes Greenwood's Ch. Violet.

PEDIGREE OF HUDDERSFIELD BEN

Sire: Mr Bascovitch's Dog	Ramsden's Bounce	Ramsden's Bob	Haighs Teddy
			Old Dolly
		Old Dolly	Albert
	Eastwoods Lady	Eastwoods Old Ben	Ramsden'Old Ben
			Young Dolly
		Young Dolly	Old Sandy
			Old Dolly
Dam: Eastwoods Lady	Eastwoods Old Ben	Ramsden's Bounce	Ramsden's Bob
			Old Dolly
		Young Dolly	Old Sandy
			Old Dolly
	Young Dolly	Old Sandy	Haigh's Teddy
			Kitty
		Old Dolly	Albert

DEVELOPING THE BREED

The Yorkshire Terrier Club was founded in 1898, after which a more detailed history of the breed was maintained. The club got a committee together to draw up a Breed Standard and the value of points to be allotted to their virtues. Although we do not judge on a points system today, it is interesting to study the points to appreciate the importance of coat and colour in the breed.

SIZE

The biggest difference between the early Yorkshire Terriers and the dogs we know today is size. The breed very quickly became much smaller towards the end of the 19th century. Originally, a Yorkshire Terrier would have weighed 12-14 lbs (5.4-6.3 kgs), and there were two classes provided, one for the under 8 lbs (3.6 kgs) and one for over that weight. The smaller Yorkies soon became popular as house pets, while the larger variety were still very popular as fearless little hunting dogs, keeping down the vermin populations in both homes and farms.

There have been a number of kennels contributing over the years to make the beautiful dog we know and love today. Mrs Walton and Mrs Beard campaigned their dogs under the Ashton prefix during the 1890s and 1900s. Their most famous dogs were Ashton King, Ashton Queen and Ashton Duke. They were thought to be excellent examples of the breed. Ashton Queen had the honour of being the bitch that won more prizes than any other living Yorkshire Terrier during its lifetime. Jack Wood of the Armley prefix made his name in the early part of the 20th century. One of his best-known Yorkies was Ch. Armley Principal Boy. Mrs W. Shaw of the Sneighton kennel also made a significant contribution.

Lady Edith Windham-Dawson of the Soham kennel was a very knowledgeable breeder and had quite a number of champions to her credit, including Ch. James of Soham, Ch. Victoria of Soham, and Ch. Rose Crystal gaining their titles between 1926 and 1939.

Another great lady of the breed was Mrs Annie Swan. Her kennel started around the 1920s and was influential until the 1950s. Her prefix of Invincia was famous for its beautiful, defined colours. She was not only a prominent breeder but was also a canine columnist for many of the leading dog journals abroad. Famous dogs carrying the Invincia prefix were Ch. Splendour of Invincia and Ch. Invincible of Invincia. Annie Swan died in 1975 aged 96.

The feature on page 25 is an article from the *Leeds Post,* published in 1921, which was among 'The Annie Swan Papers' (Annie Swan's personal collection of Yorkshire Terrier history, including all her pedigrees and memorabilia) – given and saved by David Ward (Roscommon) and Margaret Riley (Bridle), now in the possession of Rosemary Webster and Yorkshire Terrier Rescue. Our thanks to them all. I find the following article very interesting, although I think Mr Wood would today be frowned upon, as he seems to regard the dogs as more of a business than a hobby.

POINTS OF THE BREED

Formation and terrier appearance	15
Colour of hair on body	15
Richness of tan on head and legs	15
Quantity and length of coat	10
Quality of texture of coat	10
Head	10
Mouth	5
Legs and feet	5
Ears	5
Eyes	5
Tail (carriage of)	5
Total points	100

THE LEEDS SPORT POST
(Saturday 29th October 1921)

A GOOD JUDGE OF YORKSHIRE TERRIERS
Popular Breed With An Unknown Origin
By "Little John"

The origin of the Yorkshire Terrier is tied up in mystery. So said a fancier of many years when I approached him on the matter. "I've been a Yorkshireman all the time, and for the life of me I can't find how they came to be."

He talked about crosses with the Skye and the old long-haired English terrier, but knew nothing definite.

Authorities vary. One writer says that although the Yorkshire was comparatively a modern dog, he knew little about it. Once upon a time it was called the broken-haired Scotch terrier, but this was a sad misnomer. "It is suggested," he wrote, "that the Yorkshire terrier came from a very lucky combination of one of the Scottish terriers and one of the old longish-coated English terriers, and probably one with a dash of Maltese blood in it".

A fascinating and very feasible suggestion is made by another authority, who points out the possibility of the Yorkshire being a result of the visits of Paisley weavers with their dogs to the textile districts of this country.

WORTHY OF THE COUNTRY
Whatever the origin of the Yorkshire terrier, he is a worthy representative of his county. His beauty is known the civilised world over, and he is generally as game as they make 'em. The show Yorkshire terrier in his kennels is a very different gentleman to the one who struts so proudly round the show ring in his splendour. That exaggerated coat, with dark, steel blue back to contrast with the golden tan of the legs, face, head, and chest, commands respect and attention on the bench, but it looks very different when plaited or tied up in curl papers.

Have you ever seen a "Yorkshire" with his curl papers on? When I visited Mr and Mrs J. Wood, of Armley, I was introduced to Champion Armley Principal Boy, and he frisked about the house with his wonderful coat protected in curlers.

Mr Wood says the "Yorkshire" is a working man's dog. "He is a dog that requires a lot of attention if you are going to show him, and he's a dog that keeps you

Continued on page 26...

Continued from page 25...
at home. He's easy to keep, doesn't cost much in food, and can be kennelled in the house".

The Woods of Armley are well known among the Yorkshire terrier folk. They have exported dogs to America, the Colonies and foreign countries, and have shared any amount of Champions.

FINDING THEM IN THE ROUGH
Mr Wood is not a breeder. He says he has only bred one dog in his life and it was a good one. He buys litters of young puppies, sorts them out, and rears Champions. There are few better judges of a Yorkshire terrier in the rough than "Jack" Wood of Armley.

Chatting about the "Yorkshire's" coat, Mr Wood said it was the density of colour that counted. "The blue wants to be dark with a steel gleam about it, and the tan wants to be the colour of a sovereign," he said.

"We always find a plain bringing-up the best. It is careful attention and brushing that brings out the coat. The hair should at the least reach down to the floor. The 'Moustache' of one of our champions measured 26 inches across, and the hair across his back was 28 inches long. It trailed two inches when he was on the floor."

A WAR-TIME SLUMP
It is over 30 years since the Woods entered the fancy. They were hard at it for close upon ten years before they reared a Champion and since then they have had dogs that have won close upon twenty Championships (a "Championship" means that a dog must be a Champion under three different judges). Mr Wood doubts if there are so many Yorkshire terriers about nowadays as there once was. The war interfered with them to a great extent, but, he says, they are steadily making ground.

"When I entered the business," he said, " good Yorkshires cost only a matter of 15s to £1. They are a bit more than that in these times, though, of course, ordinary stuff can be got fairly cheap. You'll hear a lot about prices some dogs are fetching. That shows value of some Yorkshire terriers". Mr Wood's "that" was an advice note for a foreign bank for a sum of money close to £100.

As the prices have increased, so the Yorkshire terrier has become smaller. Where some were about 12 lb they are now about 5 lb, often less. "We have had them under 2 lb said Mrs Wood, "and they are very valuable."

VERY MUCH A TERRIER
Despite his long, silky coat and dainty appearance, the "Yorkshire" is very much a terrier. The keen terrier eyes gleam through the hair on the head, and they dance about the floor as lively as can be. They can jump many times their own height, and delight an opportunity to have a go at a rat or anything bigger," explained Mr Wood. "A friend had a dog which would go rabbiting with the best."

In other days, artificial means were used to encourage the growth of the coat. Some fanciers had special boots made, and the terrier wore these so that he should not damage his coat. The "boots" were made of a wool material or fine leather. Then there were "secret" preparations about which every Yorkshire terrier man boasted, and which were rubbed on the coat.

GROWING POPULARITY

Between 1920 and 1930, registrations for Yorkshire Terriers numbered 150-200 a year, and the breed's popularity had increased by 50 per cent by the early 1930s. Unfortunately, the Second World War all but put a stop to the showing of dogs. However, interest soon returned once the hostilities were over, and although travelling to the shows was very difficult, it did not take long for dog shows to take off again. Dogs were shown regionally to start with, but very soon managed to travel countrywide.

It was during the 1940s in Scotland that Mrs Maimee Crookshank started her famous Johnstounburn kennel. Ch. Mr Pimm of Johnstounburn was sire to seven British Champions, and the Johnstounburn strain became famous for the beautiful heads of its dogs. The affix has passed through two more sets of hands since Mrs Crookshank died.

Through the marrying of the Burghwallis and the Johnstounburn lines, the Pagnell dogs were born. This kennel, owned by Mr and Mr Groom, bred the first two dogs to go Best in Show at general Championship shows. The first was Ch. Prima Donna of Wiske (1957) followed by her brother, Ch. Pagnell Peter Pan (1961). Peter Pan went on to win the Toy group at Crufts in 1964.

Living not far away from the Pagnell kennel in Norton Pagnell, West Yorkshire, were Les and

SIGNIFICANT YORKIES

Representatives of the Soham Kennel, owned by Lady Elizabeth Windham-Dawson.

Ch. Mr Pimm of Johnstounburn.

Ch. Pagnell Peter Pan.

Ch. Jankeri Wild Child at Essandemm: Bred by Janet Redhead, owned by Susan Lucas.

Ch. Ozmilion Mystification: A Yorkshire Terrier with a remarkable show record. *Photo: Carol Ann Johnson.*

Hilda Griffiths, who owned the Beechrise affix. When Pagnell Peter Pan was mated to Beechrise Pixie, the famous Ch. Beechrise Superb was born. Superb was the sire of seven champions and Beechrise stock is known worldwide for pretty heads and good structure. The Blairsville kennel, owned by Brian and Rita Lister, was another famous kennel of the

1960s and 1970s. Their most famous dog was Ch. Blairsville Royal Seal. He was sired by Ch. Beechrise Surprise, a son of Ch. Beechrise Superb. His dam is Ch. Blairsville Most Royal. Royal Seal went on to win 50 Challenge Certificates, a breed record at that time. In addition he won 12 Best in Show at All Breed Championship Shows, 16 Reserve Best in Shows, 33 Toy

Groups and a Reserve Best in Show at Crufts in 1978.

INTO THE MODERN ERA
The only Yorkshire Terrier to win Best in Show at Crufts is Ch. Ozmilion Mystification. Mystification was bred and owned by Osman Sameja of the world-famous Ozmilion kennels. He won 50 CCs, 48 Best of Breeds, 22 Toy Groups, 9 Best in

Antaras Hot off the Press: A highly promising Yorkshire Terrier with a string of Best Puppy awards at Championship shows.

Ch. Wenwytes Without Words: Top-winning Yorkshire Terrier and Top Sire 2009.

Ch. Donnahaye Debonair: A prolific winner in the show ring, including Best in Show awards.

Show club shows, 7 Reserve Best in Show All Breed Championship shows, 3 Best in Show All Breed Championship shows, Top Yorkie 1994, Top Toy 1995, Top Dog All Breeds 1996, as well as Best in Show at Crufts 1997.

The Ozmilion kennels hold an incredible number of records in the breed, with numerous champions in this country and various parts of the world. Ch. Ozmilion Dedication was born in 1985. He was the top-winning Yorkie of all time, winning 52 CCs. Ch. Ozmilion Love in your Eyes was the top-winning bitch of all breeds in 2003. She went on to win 43 CCs in her career and several group wins.

In the Midlands, Christine Crowther (formerly Oakley) has her Candytops Kennel. All Christine's dogs go back to the Debees Kennel of Ms D. Beech. Christine's first champion was Candytops Blue Peter, made up in 1973. He produced a further four champions, one of which was Candytops Chantilly Lace. She, in turn, was mated to Blairsville Royal Seal, producing Candytops Cavalcadia, who has

Bradford Harry, an important dog in establishing the breed in America.

himself sired a further five champions. Christine's latest champion, Candytops Cosmopolitan, has 10 CCs to her credit, as well as the fabulous win of Best in Breed at Crufts 2009.

THE YORKSHIRE TERRIER IN AMERICA

Not long after the Yorkshire Terrier was recognised by the Kennel Club in Britain (1874), the first dogs were exported to the US. The first to be registered with the American Kennel Club was a little dog named Butch. He was born in 1882 and was bred by A. Webster in England and owned by Charles Andrews from Bloomington, Illinois. Mr Andrews also registered a second Yorkshire Terrier, named Daisy, born in 1884. The breeder of Daisy is unknown. The first record of an American Kennel Club champion was a dog called Bradford Harry, made a champion in 1889, four years after the breed achieved official recognition from the American Kennel Club in 1885. Bradford Harry was a descendant of the famous Huddersfield Ben.

TOP BREEDERS

The beautiful Yorkshire Terrier had quickly become a popular fashion accessory to ladies living in towns on the East and West Coast, with only a few finding their way into the mid section of the country. Interest in the breed grew, and, by the turn of the century, there were Yorkshire Terrier breeders in 21 States, although it is thought that many of the Yorkshire Terriers exhibited in America were imported from the UK. From the 1940s, when travel became more readily available, many of the top English and Irish breeders exported some of their best dogs

THE GOLDEN TOUCH

Goldie Stone was a pioneer in the breed in the United States. Goldie and her husband, Charles, both came from a circus background and performed a high-wire act until Goldie was injured and decided to retire. She had seen a Yorkshire Terrier perform in a mind-reading act, when she was watching from the wings, and decided that she would like a Yorkie. She bought a bitch called May Blossom and a stud dog named Byngo Boy from Ms Henry Riddick. These two dogs were the start of her Petite kennels. Byngo's Boy was a Champion by 1935. Goldie's main success in the 1930s was with a little dog called Ch. Petite Wee Wee whose wins totalled 20 Group placements and 20 Best of Breeds. He also won 14 Toy Groups.

PEDIGREE OF BRADFORD HARRY

Am. Ch. Bradford Harry (whelped May 16, 1885)			
	Bruce	Sandy	Bateman's Sally
			Venus
		Patterson's Minnie	
	Lady	Tyler	Huddersfied Ben
			Kitty
		Lady	

to help establish the breed in America. These immigrant Yorkshire Terriers were used extensively in breeding and in the show ring as interest in the breed expanded.

Several top winners were exported to twin sisters Miss Janet Bennett and Ms Joan Gordon of the Wildweir affix. The main basis of their stock came from Buranthea Soham, Clu-Mar and Harringay lines. Ch. Little Sir Model was the most famous of these imports, as he became the first Yorkshire Terrier to win an All-Breed Best in Show title at an American Show. This success was the start of the sisters' fantastic show career. The Wildweir kennels produced good-quality dogs, many of which became American champions. Their home-bred dog, Ch. Wildweir Pomp'N'Circumstance, sired an unbelievable 95 champions, which made him the most influential Yorkshire Terrier stud dog in America.

Myrtle Durgin started her Yorkshire Terrier Durgin kennel in St Paul, Minnesota, in 1941. Mrs Durgin was one of the original charter members of the Yorkshire Terrier Club of America (formed in 1954 and recognised by the AKC in 1958). She was also a founder member of the Land O'Lakes Kennel Club. Mrs Durgin's special love was the Brace classes. She won several Best Brace in Show awards. During her years in the breed she either bred or owned more than 20 champions with her dogs, also producing a further 30 or more champions.

Mrs Stanley Ferguson became involved in the breed in 1941 and her first Champion was made up in 1947. His name was Ch. Minikin Baby Blue. Mrs Ferguson imported the famous Ch. Star Twighlight of Clu-Mor, which she later sold to the Wildweir kennels. His litter sister, Ch. Clu-Mor Nina, went on to win five Toy Groups for Mrs Ferguson. The Mayfair kennels was established in the 1960s by Anne Soranne, who became a major influence on the breed. America and Canadian Ch. Topsy of Tolestar was her

Best in Show winner
Am. Ch. Stratford's
Magic, sire of 33
Champions.

Am. Ch. Wedgewood's Ambassador To
Love: A fine representative from the
Wedgewood Kennel now based in Florida.

WINNERS
DOG
NEW CHAMPION
MAJOR WIN
GREATER FORT MYERS
DOG CLUB
MAY 2009
DON MEYER
PHOTO

The Yorkshire Terrier has
made its mark worldwide.
This is Ch. Zue Doggy-Booms
Le Livre D'Histoire, bred and
campaigned in Sweden by
Susanne Robertsson.
Photo: Eve Robertsson.

WAR TIME HERO

During the Second World War, a Yorkshire Terrier called Smokey was found in a fox hole in New Guinea. Smokey was a tiny dog, weighing only 4 lbs (1.8 kgs). She travelled everywhere with her adopted owner, Bill Wayne, and became very popular, entertaining the troops with all the tricks she had been taught. She could be called the first therapy dog, as she visited wounded soldiers in the hospitals in Australia and New Guinea. Smokey was smuggled back to the US by Bill in an old gas-mask container, and lived as a house pet with Bill's family. Appearances on the television and the stage followed, where she was taught to ride a tiny tricycle and walked a tightrope. She was altogether a remarkable little dog who brought joy to many.

foundation bitch, who produced a number of champions for her owner.

The partnership of Anne Seranne and Barbara Wolferman began in 1966 and their Mayfair-Barban kennel has been most successful producing many champions. Their most famous dog was American and Canadian Ch. Gaytonglen Teddy of Mayfair.

American and Canadian Ch. Ce De Higgins must surely be the most famous Yorkshire Terrier in the breed's history in America. In 1978 he won the Best in Show award at the prestigious Westminster Show. He was bred and owned by Barbara and Bill Switzer.

Keeping the Yorkie flag flying in America today are top breeders and exhibitors Barbara Scott of Stratford Yorkshire Terriers (Pennsylvania) who have made up more than 60 American champions, Catherine Morris with her Wedgewood Yorkshire Terriers based in Florida, and Ava Tyree with her Tyava kennel. There are, of course, many other excellent Yorkshire Terrier breeders in America, too numerous to mention.

A YORKIE FOR YOUR LIFESTYLE

3 Chapter

A word of warning when you are contemplating choosing a Yorkshire Terrier: the dog will choose you – not the other way round! Yorkshire Terriers have so many facets to them that there is one to suit most people, whether you are young or old, active or sedentary, or whether you live in a large house with an enormous garden or an apartment in the centre of town.

MAKING THE COMMITMENT

When making the commitment to take on a Yorkshire Terrier, it is important that you are aware of the time factor involved. A Yorkie needs – sometimes demands – attention. There is no ignoring him – he will rule the roost whatever you originally planned. A Yorkshire Terrier will generally do what you would like him to

do, but will achieve it in his own way! It is important that a new owner is aware of this side of the Yorkshire Terrier; it is not that they are disobedient, just that they are such determined, intelligent little dogs.

A Yorkshire Terrier needs companionship and fun, and although he is quite able to amuse himself if left alone, it is wise not to leave him too long without something to occupy him. Yorkshire Terriers love people and I have always found that they are able to adapt, depending on the situation. A Yorkie seems to sense when to settle down and when to run riot – and even who to avoid when necessary. They love toys, slippers, cardboard rolls and newspapers, but will get anything they are able to reach if it is something different. I have Yorkshire Terriers who love pens, socks and gloves and would even

help themselves to the washing out of the tumble drier if given the opportunity.

EXERCISE REQUIREMENTS

A Yorkshire Terrier obviously needs exercise, but in this aspect they are very versatile. Many Yorkshire Terriers will walk for miles and miles, given the chance, while others do not even want to venture outside to relieve themselves, especially on a cold winter's day. However, it is important to remember that all dogs, whether large or small, need some form of exercise and a Yorkshire Terrier is no exception.

Many Yorkshire Terriers enjoy running round the garden or back yard and this is often adequate for their needs. However, walking on concrete paths helps to strengthen their muscles. It also helps to keep their nails short, as Yorkshire Terriers do not always like to have

The Yorkshire Terrier is an active dog, despite his small stature.

their nails clipped in the more traditional way. Some Yorkshire Terriers get their exercise running around the house and this is also adequate, providing the dogs go outside for fresh-air purposes at some other stage of the day. Playtime can also give Yorkshire Terriers exercise and will use up some of their boundless energy. However, it is important to remember that although Yorkshire Terriers think they are larger dogs, they are still quite petite in stature. While the terrier instinct is natural to the Yorkshire Terrier, they are better off with moderate exercise rather than great physical exertion.

WORK SCHEDULE
Your work commitment is another area that needs to be considered when taking on a Yorkshire Terrier. A Yorkie can be left alone when necessary, but will almost certainly get into mischief if left for a long period during the day. One solution to the problem of leaving a Yorkshire Terrier when you are out at work is to engage a pet sitter who will undertake the care of your dog in your absence. Alternatively, you could arrange for other family members to be around when you are not there. Dog-walking services are also generally available in most areas, which is another option to consider.

However, if your present work schedule is such that you would have to leave the dog on his own for long periods on a regular basis, perhaps you ought to reconsider having a dog until your situation changes. Bear in mind, a young dog or pup should not be left in the house for more than a couple of hours at a time without someone checking on him.

HOME SET-UP
It is important to consider safety factors with a Yorkshire Terrier; they can disappear through small apertures in fences, gates, doors or even windows. It is necessary for a garden or yard to be completely enclosed with adequate fencing or walls. Gates need to be kept closed and locked. You should ensure the gate doesn't spring back too

Showing can be an expensive – and addictive – hobby.

quickly, as it can cause immense damage to a small Yorkshire Terrier.

Areas need to be allocated in the house for sleeping, eating, and grooming. You will also need to identify areas where your Yorkshire Terrier is not permitted to go, such as beds, chairs, or sofas.

FINANCE

The cost of caring for a Yorkshire Terrier is comparable to most dog breeds, regarding medical care, vaccinations and veterinary checks. However, the cost of food is lower than for larger breeds. A Yorkshire Terrier can at times be 'finicky' with their food, but the amount they consume is much less.

The cost of equipment also needs to be taken into consideration, especially if your Yorkshire Terrier is to be a show dog. Showing can be an expensive hobby, as you will need more equipment – brushes, show boxes, covers, ribbons, leads, etc – as well as entry fees and the transport to get you to various shows around the country.

A pet owner needs to spend money on a suitable bed and blankets. A carrying case or crate is advisable for travelling. The largest cost would be to provide a safe outdoor environment for your Yorkshire Terrier, which, as previously mentioned, would need to be an adequately fenced or walled area.

YOUR NEEDS

We have looked at what a Yorkshire Terrier needs, but it is equally important to consider what you will get out of owning a Yorkshire Terrier.

First and foremost, a Yorkshire Terrier will provide you with companionship, giving affection and reliable friendship. A Yorkie does not bear grudges and will be his usual loving self no matter what mood you may be in. In fact, the Yorkshire Terrier is very sensitive to human moods, knowing when to give special affection to their owners. A Yorkshire Terrier will give his owner unconditional love at any time.

Remember, this is an intelligent dog that does not give in easily,

ROUTINE CARE

Owning a small dog such as the Yorkshire Terrier brings with it some special responsibilities. Often the dentition of Yorkshire Terriers becomes a problem, as their mouths are only small and teeth may be crowded. Therefore, it is important they are checked and cleaned regularly. A Yorkshire Terrier's nails and ears will benefit from regular trimming and checking also.

Eyes may also be a problem, as their hair may irritate them, so usually the Yorkshire Terrier's hair is fastened back with bands, ribbons or clips, or the hair is trimmed short. Regular grooming is essential if your dog is to look his best and not develop a knotted, tangled coat. Brushing also keeps the skin in good condition by the regular stimulation it receives. The good news is that Yorkshire Terriers do not moult or shed their coats, so they are often popular with people who have asthma or other allergies.

so he needs a reliable, consistent leader. Hierarchy rules with dogs, and it is therefore important that your Yorkshire Terrier does not attempt to take control and learns to live with any other dogs, cats or other animals you have within the home.

MALE OR FEMALE?
If this is to be your first dog, you may not be concerned whether you own a male or a female unless you have plans to breed a litter.

Bitches are thought by some to be calmer, quieter and easier to handle. However, a bitch will have regular seasons, which may result in restrictions regarding exercising, as this could attract the male dogs in the neighbourhood.

Males are sometimes thought to be more irritable and more likely to try to venture out on their own. There are concerns that a male may attempt to mate other animals within the home. However, most of this can be overcome with adequate training and, where appropriate, neutering can solve many problems relating to mating and/or dominance. Obviously, you would not be intending to breed from your Yorkshire Terrier if you consider neutering.

The nature of a Yorkshire Terrier often depends on whether he has been home-reared or kennel-reared. It also involves the question of training. Therefore, it is always useful to see a puppy in his own environment, and with his parents and siblings, before choosing one of your own.

FINDING A BREEDER
When you are looking for a Yorkshire Terrier, a good starting point is to contact the Kennel Club, or a local Yorkshire Terrier breed club. Be very wary of choosing a dog advertised in a local paper. While many lovely, home-reared dogs can be sourced in this way, this is also a typical outlet for puppy farmers (people who breed dogs purely for profit, with no consideration for health,

First of all you must work out what you want from your Yorkshire Terrier.

temperament or socialisation). Do your homework. Always ask to see the mother with the puppies, ask about socialisation, and try to find other dog owners who have bought from the same breeder.

There are also breed rescue sources, as well as the all-breed rescue charities, which may have puppies, youngsters or adults available.

QUESTIONS TO ASK

When you have located a breeder, there are a number of important questions to ask, which include the following:

- Are both parents pedigree dogs and registered with the Kennel Club?
- How many are in the litter?
- Are both males and females available?
- What age are the puppies?

- When will they be ready to go to their new homes?
- Are the puppies home-reared or kennel-reared?
- What socialisation have they had?
- Have the puppies been vaccinated and wormed?
- If you are looking for a show dog, are there puppies with show potential in the litter?
- What price are the puppies?

HOME-REARED OR KENNEL-REARED?

Depending on the breeder you choose, the puppies may be reared in the family home or in a kennel environment. Home-reared Yorkshire Terriers have a tendency to be more easily integrated into a family environment and usually socialise more easily. But this does depend on the socialisation programme of the breeder. If a puppy has been brought up getting used to different people and amidst the general noise of a busy household, he is unlikely to shy away from new contacts. Kennel-reared Yorkshire Terriers may be equally sociable if they have come into contact with lots of different people, but you should talk to the breeder and find out how much socialisation the puppies have received.

ASSESSING THE PUPPIES

Yorkshire Terrier puppies are irresistible, but you need to keep a cool head and try to assess the puppies as objectively as possible. In the first instance, you need to take note of the environment in which the puppies have been reared.

Regardless of whether the puppies have been reared in the home or a kennel, their living quarters should be clean. There should be a supply of fresh water available and clean, fresh bedding at all times. The puppies should appear bright-eyed and inquisitive. While it may be natural for them to be shy and a bit cautious before approaching you, they should not appear unduly scared or uninterested. Check around the eyes, ears and anus. The presence of any discharge is something you need to be wary of.

Since April 2007 the Yorkshire Terrier, along with other breeds, has been banned from having his tail docked in the UK. Therefore, the puppies you see should all have intact tails. However, it is

You need to find a breeder that has a reputation for producing, Yorkshire Terrier puppies that are typical of the breed and are sound in mind and body.

still routine practice for many breeders to have the vet remove a puppy's dewclaws at a few days of age. Therefore, do not be surprised if the puppy has no dewclaws.

VIEWING THE LITTER

Most Yorkshire Terrier litters vary between one and four puppies. If the litter is larger, it will generally mean that the puppies have not been cared for entirely by the mother and they may have needed supplementary feeding by the breeder. It may also mean the mother has had to use a immense amount of energy and nutritional resources to rear her puppies, so it is useful to know if she needed any supplements or treatment herself. Many Yorkshire Terrier mothers give their heart and soul to rearing a litter, regardless of the number of puppies, leaving their own bodies very much depleted.

It is advisable to see the mother, and siblings if possible, of the Yorkshire Terrier you hope to take home, to ascertain how they react together. The temperament of the mother should give you some indication of the puppies' temperament. The size of each can be observed and you can assess whether they

Try not to let your heart rule your head when you are choosing a puppy.

are all of similar size or whether there is an immense variation from tiny to large. It is unlikely you will be able to see the sire of a litter unless the breeder has used her own dog. If this is the case, it is important to see the pedigree of the litter to ensure there has not been excessive inbreeding, as this could enhance any genetic faults and problems in the litter. Most pedigrees should indicate at least three generations, so it is easy to identify whether close-breeding has occurred. A father/daughter, mother/son, or brother/sister breeding is not advisable and litters from these alliances are best avoided.

By viewing the puppies in their usual environment it is possible and helpful to ascertain their temperament to some extent – whether they are dominant and bossy or quiet and retiring. I have known shy Yorkshire

Terriers become more outgoing once their dominant sibling has left the litter, so it is useful to observe them at play for a short while.

A Yorkshire Terrier brood bitch generally makes a very good mother and spends a long time feeding, cleaning and organising her litter, as she is a very proud mother as a rule. It is also a good idea to see how the mother responds to her puppies; whether she favours one or another or treats them fairly. Sometimes the mother will encourage a quiet one and try to subdue a more boisterous one, but this also depends on the characteristics and temperament of the mother.

Sometimes the mother will not allow her puppies to be touched, or even viewed. It is important that the prospective owner respects this, as a Yorkshire Terrier mother can become quite

possessive at times, even to the extent of picking up her puppy and taking him out of sight and burying him under the blankets. It is always wise to be guided by the breeder, as he or she generally should know the brood bitch well enough to know how she will react. If a brood bitch is confident that her pups will come to no harm, she may allow the buyer to view or touch a new puppy, providing the breeder holds the pup within her sight and reach.

Most puppies are ready to leave their mothers at about 8-10 weeks if they are going to a pet home. However, a show prospect may not be ready until 3-4 months. It all depends on the type of home the puppy is going to. Obviously, the older the pup, the more likely he is to have had his vaccinations, but this will be discussed in a later chapter (see Chapter Eight).

It is important to see the mother with her puppies so you can get an idea of the temperament they are likely to inherit.

You need to be completely honest with the breeder so you can find the puppy that will suit your lifestyle.

CHOOSING A PET

As a companion, a puppy needs to be friendly, affectionate, sociable, and enjoy people and company. He should be neither too boisterous nor too quiet. If an elderly couple take on a very boisterous puppy, they may find it difficult to manage, but often a Yorkshire Terrier will adapt to their needs through training. If the pup is to go to a very boisterous family home, he needs to be outgoing and able to cope with the noise and bustle of family life.

A Yorkshire Terrier will learn quickly what he can and cannot do, but he will also attempt to get his own way (and usually succeed) as to which chair he can occupy, etc. It takes a very strong, determined owner to stop this happening, one who has set him or herself up as pack leader (see Chapter Six).

The Yorkshire Terrier knows rules and how to flout them, but he is a loving companion and friend who cares when you are 'under the weather' or feeling 'down at heart' and is always there to cheer you up when you need it. A Yorkshire Terrier knows when the postman or visitors call before they even reach the door, and they make excellent guard dogs. They would protect their owners to the death if need be, I am sure.

The golden rule here is to be honest with the breeder. The more the breeder knows about you and your lifestyle, the more likely it is that you will end up with the right puppy for your household.

If a pup has not quite reached the ideal quality for showing, it is possible that the breeder will let you have him as a pet. Such puppies often make ideal pets, although they may be a little older than the usual new puppy (about 3-4 months rather than 8-10 weeks, for example). However, if a pup has an obvious defect that may affect his quality of life, the breeder has an obligation to inform you about it, especially if the pup is likely to need surgical treatment or have a shortened life-span.

AN OLDER DOG

Choosing an adult Yorkshire Terrier is an option for some potential owners, who perhaps do not have the opportunity or facilities to train a young puppy. A more elderly owner would probably prefer an older dog who is less active, more settled, trained and hopefully more obedient than a very young puppy. Or it may be that time is a factor and the potential owner just does not have the time to spend training a young puppy.

It is important to understand that although Yorkshire Terriers appear small and fragile, they actually are quite robust in nature and often live to the age of 15 years or even more. Even if you are taking on an adult dog, you need to be prepared to provide him with a home for many years.

Whatever the reason for taking on an older Yorkie, it is important that the owner knows the characteristics of the adult dog, who will no doubt have acquired some traits and habits that he expects to continue. Diet may be a problem with an adult dog, as he generally becomes

SHOW PROSPECT

If you intend to show your Yorkshire Terrier, it is vital that you tell the breeder this in advance. Most show breeders will keep the best of the litter for themselves, but if other puppies are going to be sold for show purposes, they will generally be of good quality. You should be aware that it is not always possible to predict whether a puppy will be of show quality until he is considerably older than the age at which most pet puppies leave the mother. A show Yorkshire Terrier would generally be obtained at a later age than a pet, as it is more likely that the size, colour, temperament, conformation and movement is identified.

The colour of a Yorkshire Terrier varies with the dog's maturity. A puppy is born with hair that is black and tan while in adulthood it ideally becomes steel blue and tan with a silky textured coat (although some Yorkshire Terriers may be steel grey and tan or even silver and tan). The tan should ideally consist of three different shades. A puppy has short hair initially, and many pet owners keep the hair trimmed for convenience, but an adult show Yorkshire Terrier has long, flowing hair that gives him a very

elegant appearance.

Show Yorkshire Terriers need to be of a steady temperament but with an extra vivacity that is difficult to describe but obvious when you see it in a show dog. A show dog needs to be sound, both in body and mind. A show Yorkshire Terrier has to be able to stand for varying periods on the box in the show ring, while other dogs are alongside, without getting aggressive, distressed, restless or bored. A show Yorkshire Terrier also has to be handled by the judge on a table without jumping off or getting distressed. The show dog then has to walk on a lead up and down the ring under the scrutiny of the judge and then stand back on the box.

Preparation for showing is somewhat extreme for the Yorkie, involving oiling, 'crackering', brushing, trimming, bathing and handling. A successful show dog needs to have a patient, obedient and even temperament. He also needs a strong, confident disposition if he is to enjoy exhibiting and showing off in the ring.

Along with these characteristics, the show Yorkshire Terrier must also be a good traveller. It is no use having a Yorkshire Terrier who is car-

used to certain types of food. An adult Yorkshire Terrier may have problems with teeth, especially if elderly, so diet could be important from this aspect also.

An adult Yorkshire Terrier may have a trimmed coat or may be a retired show dog with a long coat, so it is useful to decide whether to allow the coat to grow or trim it to a more manageable length (which is generally advisable for a pet). An adult Yorkshire Terrier should have an up-to-date vaccination record and be trained to some degree, as well as able to walk on a lead.

A very elderly Yorkshire Terrier may not be very active and will simply enjoy pottering around the home in a very leisurely way. He may not be too happy if boisterous youngsters are around and may prefer to disappear to his bed at these times.

If an adult dog is being

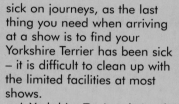

sick on journeys, as the last thing you need when arriving at a show is to find your Yorkshire Terrier has been sick – it is difficult to clean up with the limited facilities at most shows.

A Yorkshire Terrier obviously needs to be restrained during travelling and most people use the carrying box that the dog is shown on, or a wire cage/crate, either of which needs to be safely attached to the car-seat with a safety-harness. There are various harnesses available for dogs travelling in cars, but I believe the cage or box to be the safest – it is important to remember that if an accident occurs, the small, light-weight Yorkshire Terrier will not have a chance of surviving if he is not safely secured.

It takes an expert eye to evaluate show potential.

integrated into a home with young Yorkshire Terriers or other pets, it is essential to handle the introductions with sensitivity and patience. It is important not to upset the status of the resident dog but to allow the hierarchy to adjust naturally. This also applies when introducing a new puppy into a home with an adult Yorkshire Terrier, though puppies are generally more passive with adult dogs and tend to fit in more easily.

RESCUED DOGS

Rescued dogs are generally adult dogs who need rehoming for whatever reason. It is helpful, if possible, to know what the situation has been. Most dogs are in centres through no fault of their own (such as bereavement or family breakdown), and these dogs make wonderful pets when given the opportunity to settle into a new home.

If a Yorkshire Terrier has become orphaned as a puppy, he generally will adopt a mother and siblings quite easily. However, an adult dog that has lost his owner will generally pine for them quite strongly and mope around for some time before accepting a new owner, so it is important that the new owner understands this and does not feel the Yorkshire Terrier does not want to belong to them. Yorkshire Terriers love to belong to people and the loss of an owner can be a tremendous shock to such a devoted dog. A new owner

needs to be patient with a rescued dog to gain his trust and devotion. A Yorkshire Terrier that has been ill-treated or been through some sort of shock needs even more time, patience, and understanding.

Taking on a rescued Yorkshire Terrier is not an easy option. Prospective owners will be thoroughly vetted to ensure the right match of dog and owner is made. Nor is it a cheap option. Most organisations will ask for a donation to cover the costs of caring for the dog up until that point (which may include a complete course of vaccinations).

Large rehoming organisations, such as Dogs Trust, may have Yorkshire Terriers available, and the Yorkshire Terrier breed rescue

It may suit your lifestyle to miss out on the puppy stage and take on an older dog.

societies also provide rehoming for Yorkshire Terriers rescued from extreme situations, such as destruction of kennels through fire, bereavement of owners, rescue from extremely overcrowded or neglectful kennels, as well as the equivalent of temporary fostering while owners are hospitalised for ill-health.

The Yorkshire Terrier rescue societies are self-funding and donations are gratefully received. Various members of the breed clubs offer temporary homes to rescued Yorkshire Terriers at extremely short notice until more permanent homes are found, and obviously these are vetted for their suitability to take a rescued Yorkshire Terrier into their homes.

If you are able to offer plenty of time and patience to care for a Yorkie in need of a new home, your rescued dog will bring a new dimension to your life and reward you with lifelong companionship and devotion.

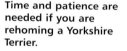

Time and patience are needed if you are rehoming a Yorkshire Terrier.

THE NEW ARRIVAL

Chapter 4

Whether your new Yorkshire Terrier is a puppy, an adult or even a rescued dog, it is important to establish a few ground rules so that your Yorkie (and you) are left in no doubt as to who is the 'pack leader' (see Chapter Six). A Yorkshire Terrier is intelligent enough to understand that you are in charge and although he may rebel against many of your instructions during training, he will respect you more if you remain 'the boss'! The Yorkshire Terrier (as with other breeds) needs to know that you are the leader in the household hierarchy, and, providing you are consistent, your dog will live within the guidelines you set. Of course, a Yorkshire Terrier also knows how to get his own way and how to escape, so this may be a challenge that you, the owner, have to be ready to face at some point in the future.

HOME & GARDEN

It's vital to provide a safe environment for your Yorkshire Terrier. A Yorkshire Terrier can escape through very small spaces, so it is important that your garden or yard does not have any gaps that your Yorkie could slip through. The initial outlay of preventing this may be expensive, but as an alternative to losing your Yorkshire Terrier, or his being injured or killed, it is well worth it.

It is also essential that your Yorkshire Terrier has his own area for sleeping, eating and exercise. Sometimes a Yorkshire Terrier is permitted to sleep on a new owner's bed to settle in initially, but be warned: your Yorkshire Terrier will come to expect that every time. Once established, this will be a difficult habit to break. A separate area for sleeping is useful for a Yorkshire Terrier, because although they can be very active dogs, they also like to have their own 'chill-out' area that they can retire to when requiring peace and quiet from family life.

An eating area is important, so your dog knows where he can obtain fresh water when needed and where his meals will be found. Remember that human and animal dishes should always be stored separately, for hygiene purposes.

An exercise area for your Yorkshire Terrier should also be provided, and it is useful for a new arrival to identify a specific area where he can let off steam or relieve himself in order to get into some sort of routine, which most Yorkshire Terriers seem to thrive on, as they are very much creatures of habit.

Specific garden areas need to

An inquisitive Yorkshire Terrier puppy will want to explore every nook and cranny of his new home.

be identified for your Yorkshire Terrier to use for both toilet and exercise purposes, as well as no-go areas. By fencing in the allowed area you can protect the rest of your garden from damage from your Yorkshire Terrier. However a Yorkshire Terrier, if so inclined, is able to jump a fair height. I've known them jump over three feet (91 cms) high, so your fencing needs to be adequate to contain them.

BUYING EQUIPMENT

Your Yorkshire Terrier will need a number of items that you should buy in advance of his arrival. Pet shops have baskets, bedding, toys and food of varying types and many supermarkets have pet foods and equipment available at reasonable prices. Other

alternative sources include dog shows, where you may often obtain items on special offer, the internet (though do your homework to ensure you are buying good quality), and possibly even your Yorkie's breeder. Usually, the breeder (or previous owner) can pass on their sources, especially regarding food stockists, and will guide you as to the size of bed needed.

BED AND BEDDING

Your Yorkshire Terrier needs a bed of some sort. A small bed is obviously needed for a Yorkshire Terrier, as he likes to be snug and cosy, but it still needs to allow your dog to move around and shuffle his blankets about, so the very smallest size is often

too small. It is best to measure against the dog first.

Dog beds can be soft, padded beds, hard-plastic beds with lots of soft bedding, quilted fleeces or baskets with plenty of covers and padding. Sometimes newspapers can give added protection under the bedding and add to the insulation of the bed as well as absorbing accidents. Baskets generally are not really suitable for Yorkshire Terriers, as although they look good, the basket weave can play havoc with their coats and most puppies also quite enjoy chewing them. Whatever bed you choose, it is important that it is placed in a draught-proof area and accessible for your Yorkshire Terrier throughout the day.

Padded quilts and fleece blankets to line the bed seem to suit Yorkshire Terriers quite well, as they can snuggle down into them and pull them around to make a cosy nest. Any bedding used for your Yorkshire Terrier obviously needs to be washable and any type of bed used needs to be regularly cleaned and disinfected.

Bedding can be fleece or quilted or even old jumpers or coats (which obviously need the buttons or fasteners removing first) or you may be able to make blankets and bedding yourself if you are handy with a needle. The cost of most bedding is fairly reasonable, although some sources seem to charge exorbitant prices for branded goods. It is your choice.

A crate or carrier will keep your puppy safe when you are travelling.

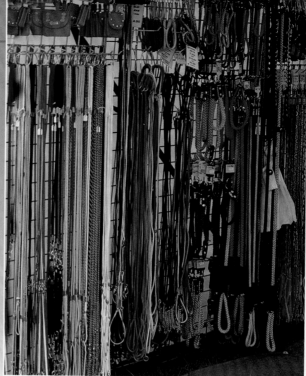

You will find a wide variety of collars and leads for sale if you visit a dog show.

CRATES/BOXES

A crate or cage is a good idea if you need to confine your dog to a specific area. As long as you do not use the crate or cage as a punishment area, your dog will generally be happy to retire there when you are at work, when guests deem it necessary, to house your dog overnight, or for travelling in the car. Size is important in order to allow the Yorkshire Terrier to move around comfortably inside. You also need to consider whether it will fold flat or remain intact, in which case storage space needs to be considered.

Carrying boxes or show boxes tend to be smaller than the crate but are equally useful for transporting your Yorkshire Terrier around for short periods. A show box is not ideal for long periods or overnight, as there is not as much space for the Yorkshire Terrier to move around in. One advantage of a crate is that food and water dishes can be clipped on to the sides.

COLLAR AND LEAD

A Yorkshire Terrier will also need a collar and lead. Many of the collars on sale are for medium to large dogs, and it is often difficult to obtain one suitable for a Yorkshire Terrier. Cat collars are generally about the right size but are usually not very strong and only really suitable for younger puppies. A harness could be useful, but again there are few small enough for a small Yorkshire Terrier.

Leather ferret collars seem to be the right size for Yorkshire Terriers, or, alternatively, the slip-leads made of nylon, which are used for showing. Dog shows are the places for the very small collars and leads, though pet stores do stock some small sizes or will obtain them for you. The

Your puppy will enjoy having toys to play with, but you must ensure that they are 100 per cent safe.

internet is another source. If a collar has a buckle on, it is important to check that it does not become tangled up in your Yorkshire Terrier's hair, as this could be extremely uncomfortable for him.

GROOMING EQUIPMENT

Grooming gear for your Yorkshire Terrier is important if he is to look his best and his coat and skin are to be kept in good condition. This means at least a brush and comb. Bobbles and bands are generally used to keep a Yorkshire Terrier's hair out of his eyes and off his face, and these can be obtained at supermarkets or chemists. A show Yorkshire Terrier would need ribbons and bows as well as the bands or clips. A grooming table is useful but not essential, but remember that daily grooming is a must to keep your Yorkshire Terrier looking good. Nail clippers, scissors, toothbrushes and shampoos will also be needed to keep your Yorkie well groomed.

TOYS

Toys are quite important for Yorkshire Terriers and help them use up some of their boundless terrier energy. Obviously, very small toys are more in keeping with a Yorkshire Terrier, though he will also enjoy playing with gigantic teddies if given the opportunity to do so. It is important that you decide which toys your dog can or cannot have. Be as rigorous as if you were choosing a toy for a child under the age of three. Any easily removable small parts are choking hazards. Poor-quality stitching on a soft toy is an open invitation for the toy to be ripped open, exposing the stuffing, which can be fatal if swallowed.

Yorkshire Terriers do seem to like squeaky toys (even though you may not appreciate the continuous noise squeaking after a while). Knotted rope toys or knotted tights make good tug-of-war toys for Yorkshire Terriers, and cardboard tubes seem to make suitable toys for them to chew or shred.

Slippers, socks and gloves make interesting toys for them, if they can get hold of them, so keep these items out of reach if you value them!

FOOD AND FEEDING BOWLS

Dishes for food and water are necessary when taking a Yorkshire Terrier into your home. Although plastic dishes are colourful, they soon become damaged when your Yorkshire Terrier's teeth develop, and the ragged edges of the chewed dishes can easily damage the Yorkshire Terrier's facial hair. Stainless-steel dishes generally are the best to use and are easily washed and dried. Crockery is less sturdy when your Yorkshire Terrier has finished eating and may upturn the dish. Saucers or shallow dishes tend to be ideal for puppies, as they allow easier access to the food. A shallow dish is useful for fresh water, which needs to be available throughout the day for your dog. Larger dishes are often difficult for a Yorkshire Terrier to reach into for eating, so it is better to use the small to medium-small sizes.

It is important to find out what your new dog is accustomed to eating. Initially, try to maintain a similar diet to that provided by the previous owner/breeder. He or she should provide you with a diet sheet or information that identifies the dog's previous diet pattern. Follow this for the first few weeks, until your new Yorkie has settled in. You can change your dog's diet if you choose, but a new pet has a lot of adjustments to make and changing his diet straight away is an unnecessary extra to contend with at this time.

FINDING A VET

Finding a veterinary surgeon can be easy if you know other people with Yorkshire Terriers in your area, as they generally recommend someone who is used to caring for small animals, Yorkshire Terriers in particular. If not, the breeder may be able to recommend one.

It is useful to visit the selected veterinary surgery and see for yourself what care they give and what facilities they provide. If you do not feel happy about the veterinary surgery, do not entrust your Yorkshire Terrier to them. Remember that you would not leave a friend or family member under the care of someone you did not trust, so you should consider the same treatment for your pet.

Once you are happy with your choice of veterinary surgery, you should register and take your dog along for an introductory check-up. The vet will probably wish to examine your Yorkshire Terrier to ensure he is fit, well and up to date with all the necessary vaccinations, as well as advising you on routine health care, such as worming.

Stainless steel bowls are easy to clean, and they are virtually indestructible.

IDENTIFICATION

Identification is generally in the form of a disc on the collar around the Yorkshire Terrier's neck, which should give the owner's surname and address; many people also give a phone number. Microchipping and tattooing is the most modern option of identification, which can be carried out at your veterinary surgery. A tag ID is a legal requirement for dogs in the UK.

After the long wait, at last it is time to collect your puppy.

do this yourself if you are driving.

It is advisable for your puppy not to have eaten a meal immediately prior to travelling and for you to have sufficient materials in the vehicle in case of an accident. Wet-wipes, clean blankets, paper towels and plastic bags for soiled articles will be useful.

The car needs to be a comfortable temperature for your puppy, not too cold and not too warm, with adequate ventilation on a hot day. Air-conditioning in the car is ideal for most dogs, although a Yorkshire Terrier in a small travelling box in a car could still get quite overheated so be aware of this if the journey is more than an hour or two.

FOOD & DIET SHEET

A breeder will normally give you a diet sheet containing details of what the puppy has been fed and how often. It is customary for the breeder to give the new owner sufficient food for the next few meals so that changes are not necessary straight away, and it is useful to know where to obtain further supplies. It is helpful if the breeder has already given the puppy a variety of foods, as this allows him to have experienced different tastes and textures. The puppy should also be used to drinking fresh water (available at all times), not milk, by the time he leaves the breeder. It is important that the puppy is only given puppy food, dried or moist, as this is specially formulated for a puppy's

COLLECTING YOUR PUPPY

Collecting a pet can be traumatic for you and your family as well as for the Yorkshire Terrier himself. Preparation is the key to making this as smooth as possible. Generally a puppy will be collected by car and it is essential that you have some cage or travel box for your puppy to travel in. A second person is necessary to support and reassure your puppy during the journey home, as you cannot

PAPERWORK

When collecting your puppy from the breeder, there will be an exchange of paperwork. You may have to sign a contract with the breeder (this will have been discussed in advance, if relevant), and you will be given registration documents. insurance documents (if any – the Kennel Club usually provide six weeks' free insurance for new owners registering puppies with them), the dog's pedigree certificate, the relevant health records, and the dietary details. The registration documents will show the legal details of your puppy, name, registration number, date of birth, breeder and previous owner, the dam and sire of the puppy, and information regarding transferring ownership of the puppy to yourself. The breeder should explain the procedure and complete and sign the relevant sections of the form.

Some breeders do not give the registration documents when a puppy is going to be a pet, but this should have been negotiated prior to collecting the puppy. If there is going to be some delay in obtaining this document, there should be an adequate explanation from the breeder – sometimes it is merely because of a delay in naming a puppy. The registration documents are needed for you to transfer ownership of the puppy so are essential if you intend to show, breed or use your pup for stud in the future.

The pedigree of your puppy should be given to you also, although this can be obtained on request from the Kennel Club. Most new owners like to be made aware of the pedigree of their puppy prior to sale. The Kennel Club will insure a new puppy free for the first six weeks, on transfer of ownership and registration with them, so it is essential to receive the relevant documentation to do this.

Health records of the puppy or adult are important so that you know what vaccinations he has had and the dates they were given, or, alternatively, with a very young puppy, when they are due to commence. There should be a verbal communication with the breeder regarding whether and when the puppy has been wormed or given any other treatment or medication during his life. Obviously, if you are taking an older dog, it is essential that you have documentation regarding regular vaccinations so you know when they are next due.

digestion. Adult food is not suitable.

Puppy care information leaflets or booklets are often given to new owners, but this is at the breeder's discretion. However, these leaflets can be obtained by post from the various dog food manufacturers or on the internet.

If you need to change the dog's food, you can choose between dried complete food, moist manufactured food in sachets or tins, and mixer food (biscuits usually fed with canned meat), all of which are suitable for a Yorkshire Terrier (see Chapter Five). Yorkshire Terriers tend to have quite 'finicky' appetites at times, but at others he will eat for England; it is often a matter of seeing what he likes eating best.

Obviously, like many other breeds, Yorkshire Terriers will eat anything they are not supposed to, but that must also be at your discretion. It is very inadvisable to give your Yorkshire Terrier pork, as his digestion cannot tolerate it. Most Yorkshire Terriers like chicken, beef and lamb but will usually need to have supplements if only given fresh meat. Dried complete foods should supply all the necessary components and nutrients for a puppy and adult dog alike.

The problem for Yorkshire Terriers is that if eating dried food, it needs to be small enough for them to eat – some dried food is far too large for Yorkshire Terriers. Some food companies produce small-sized food for small dogs. The mixers that also come in small-bite size are suitable for Yorkshire Terriers, and moist food can obviously be given, regardless of the dog's size, although quantities must be assessed according to what each Yorkshire Terrier's requirements are.

MEETING THE FAMILY

Meeting the family should be a gradual process, although some puppies may have been reared in busy family homes and already be used to numerous people being around. The puppy needs to identify who his new owner is and who is going to be the 'pack leader' (see Chapter Six); too many people around at the same time could simply overwhelm a small Yorkshire Terrier puppy. It is important to remember the size of a Yorkshire Terrier; even though they appear fearless, they need to feel safe and secure when leaving their mother and siblings behind and going into a new, strange environment.

CHILDREN

Children need to be aware that the Yorkshire Terrier puppy needs to be treated with respect and gentleness. Children need to understand that they should not become cross or angry with a puppy if he does not respond to them initially. Children should be taught how to handle and lift a Yorkshire Terrier puppy safely and to be aware that the puppy is still a baby and could easily be injured if dropped. Children often love a Yorkshire Terrier, because he is so small, but they are not always aware of how wriggly he can be. Likewise, the Yorkshire Terrier needs to be

Make sure you take note of all the instructions regarding the care of your new puppy.

Supervise all interactions with children and then relations will start on a good footing.

taught to treat younger members of the human pack with respect. He must be shown how to be gentle with young children. He should not be left alone unsupervised with small children.

Mouthing can be a problem with Yorkshire Terriers (as well as other dogs). It is vital that this is discouraged. No members of the household must allow the puppy to chew their fingers.

RESIDENT DOGS

Other dogs need to be introduced carefully. A new puppy is often easier to introduce into a home with a dog than an adult Yorkshire Terrier, but it depend on the characteristics of the original dog at home. Respect the hierarchy already in place. Supervise first interactions carefully until you know that the dogs will get along well together. While it is understandable that you will want to lavish attention on your new Yorkie, make sure that you do not leave the resident dog feeling left out, as this may inadvertently encourage problems between him and the new arrival.

When out walking your Yorkshire Terrier, it is important to understand that he sees himself as much larger than he really is and he will have little fear of large dogs. A Yorkie is generally friendly and will want to greet all other dogs, but it is important that you do not allow this unless the other owner agrees, as a Yorkshire Terrier may be badly injured by over-enthusiastic play with a larger or aggressive dog.

YORKSHIRE TERRIER

A Yorkshire Terrier can learn to live in harmony with a cat, but you will need to supervise their first meetings.

OTHER PETS

Other pets again need to be introduced gradually. To begin with, it is best to keep the Yorkie restrained on a lead when introducing a cat or other pet. Never leave your Yorkie alone with another pet until you are sure he is reliable. A Yorkshire Terrier has a strong chase instinct – remember, he is basically a hunting terrier, albeit a small one – therefore, you will need to be consistent about discouraging this type of response. A strong, firm "No!" every time he goes to chase a cat, for example, is essential.

SETTLING IN

Settling in needs care, time and patience, so if you work, it is best to arrange time off so that you can give the necessary attention to your Yorkshire Terrier during this crucial period. Remember that it will feel strange and overwhelming for a new puppy just leaving his mother and siblings. He may find it distressing and lonely if left on his own. An older Yorkshire Terrier may adapt much more easily, but again, he may become disorientated and distressed, especially if he is a rescue dog who has probably

had enough changes to his life already. An unsettled Yorkshire Terrier may rebel if confined to one area and destroy or damage surroundings or furniture, so it is important that someone remains with him to reassure him and calm him down if he does show any sign of distress. However, it is also important that you do not overwhelm your new arrival. Your Yorkshire Terrier needs to know the area where he can find peace and quiet (e.g. his own bed), and be left alone, and you should respect that desire to be left alone.

THE FIRST NIGHT

The first night can be difficult for the Yorkshire Terrier and new owner alike, and, again, time and patience are necessary. Make sure you have a comfortable bed and blankets for your Yorkshire Terrier, and, after playing with him and allowing him to relieve himself, try to settle him down for a sleep. It is important the area is not draughty or noisy, and it's advisable that the breeder sends either a blanket or a toy with the Yorkshire Terrier so that he has something familiar to snuggle up with.

The first night can be quite traumatic and noisy. The owner must be prepared to constantly settle and reassure the new Yorkshire Terrier puppy. It is no use getting cross with him. This is a contentious issue, with some people advocating leaving the new puppy to howl or bark so that he learns to sleep through the night without you, but ultimately it is your choice. If you give in and let him sleep on your bed, you will end up with a habit difficult to break, but if you don't mind a sleeping companion, then this may be the best choice for you. Whatever option you choose, remember that you are setting up a life-long habit, so don't allow anything now that you will not be happy to tolerate in a year's time.

CRATE TRAINING

Crate training can be commenced once the Yorkshire Terrier is familiar with his territory. Encourage him to go into the crate for short periods of time, leaving the door open to begin with. With his own blanket and toys inside, together with water and some food, the Yorkshire Terrier will often explore the cage himself. If the door remains open, the Yorkshire Terrier will treat the crate as his own special den, perhaps sleeping or eating in there completely voluntarily. When he appears settled, the door can be closed for short periods of time, lengthening it gradually. Do not use the crate for punishment or leave your puppy inside for more than four hours at a time (except for overnight).

HOUSE TRAINING

It is important that your puppy has had the chance to relieve himself prior to settling down for the night, and that he knows where to go or what to use if needing the toilet during the night. It is generally advisable to put newspapers down on the floor near the bed and outside

If you reassure your puppy when he is first introduced to his crate, he will soon learn to settle in it.

59

If you establish a routine of taking your puppy out at regular intervals, it will not be long before he is clean in the house.

the door overnight. Also ensure that your Yorkshire Terrier puppy does not have access to other rooms during the night, as he may use other areas for toilet purposes. A dog hates to soil in his sleeping area, so do not assume that a Yorkie caught short will confine the mess to where he is housed overnight. If he is allowed access elsewhere, he will try to mess as far away from his bed as possible. If you are faced with an accident, do not get cross. Your puppy cannot help it any more than a baby in nappies can help soiling himself.

A Yorkshire Terrier usually learns to be clean very quickly and will, in time, ask to go out, not necessarily by barking but by

emphasising the need to go out of the back door, generally running backwards and forwards and looking at you until you realise. A Yorkshire Terrier needs to know which area to use in the garden or yard and should be allowed to go out in the morning on waking, after eating, and at various times during the day. I would say every two to three hours is probably a good idea with a puppy. It is important that you praise your puppy when he has achieved the desired result and encourage the positive results while trying to ignore the negative ones.

A Yorkshire Terrier responds well to treats after successful toileting, but beware you do not

encourage him to do tiny efforts in a bid to get more treats – Yorkies can be quite devious in this respect! Obviously, if accidents occur in the home, it is better simply to put the dog outside and emphasise where he should go; it is no use getting angry, as it will simply make him more anxious and more likely to have accidents indoors when getting stressed.

HOUSE RULES
House rules depend very much on yourself and what you want from your Yorkshire Terrier. He will claim chairs, beds, rooms and belongings if at all possible, so it is up to you to emphasise that he should not jump up on

HANDLING

Accustom your puppy to being handled from an early age so he is ready to accept grooming, and examination by a vet when necessary.

Pick up each paw in turn.

Examine the ears.

Open the mouth to check the teeth and gums.

to the bed or chair and that he does not go upstairs. Obviously, a baby's cot and pram must be out of bounds for any dog, and a Yorkshire Terrier is no exception. A Yorkshire Terrier should be encouraged to know that a baby comes above him in the hierarchy stakes and that he is not allowed near the baby or in his room. A Yorkshire Terrier will stand guard over a baby and be very protective, but be aware that he could suffocate a baby if allowed in the pram.

The Yorkshire Terrier also quickly learns that he should return to his basket or bed while his owners are eating and should not be encouraged to approach the table at meal times.

With a small breed, such as the Yorkie, it is tempting to allow certain behaviours that would not be tolerated in a larger dog. To some extent, this is a matter of personal preference. However, remember that, regardless of size, your Yorkie is a dog, not a person. Therefore, to avoid future problems, it is vital that you establish your authority over your dog, even if you do decide to allow him on the sofa (see Chapter Six).

HANDLING AND GROOMING

Grooming is important not only to keep the coat in good condition, but also to keep the skin healthy and to reinforce the

'pack' hierarchy and cement the bond between dog and owner. First experiences can be frightening but exciting for a Yorkshire Terrier and need to be dealt with carefully. It is much easier to start as you mean to go on. A Yorkshire Terrier who has been handled as a puppy will grow up not only to tolerate grooming, but to actively enjoy it. Therefore, from the moment you bring home your new puppy, encourage him to be petted, handled and brushed, to build up the length of time he will accept grooming. It's far better to start off with positive five-minute sessions that can be built on, than attempting a marathon hour and giving up halfway through.

A puppy has a lot to learn when he arrives in his new home, but if you establish the house rules so he understands what is required, he will soon become an integral member of the family.

The dog should be encouraged to stand still for grooming sessions and while bands are put in his hair. He should allow his owner to check his eyes, ears and mouth, as well as allowing his teeth to be inspected and cleaned. The nails of a Yorkshire Terrier can grow fairly rapidly so will need regular trimming. This also requires your Yorkie to stand still long enough for you to check and trim the nails. Holding a Yorkshire Terrier in order to trim his nails can be difficult if he struggles and wriggles, but, with practice and patience, he will get used to the handling. The owner must be firm and consistent, otherwise the Yorkshire Terrier will struggle all the more and it will often become a battleground.

A show Yorkshire Terrier needs his ears, feet and coat trimming to show standards, but a pet Yorkshire Terrier can have his coat trimmed much shorter for the convenience of the owner and to prevent the coat from tangling. The ears can still be trimmed, but many pet owners do not worry about this. A show Yorkshire Terrier also needs to get used to the idea of bathing and brushing prior to going to a show.

Handling is an extension of what is required for grooming. All-over handling can be practised and carried out at ring-craft training sessions whereby potential trainers 'go over' the dogs and get them to walk on a lead and to stand on their boxes or table. Most show Yorkshire Terriers take to this very well and thoroughly enjoy the occasion. Pet Yorkshire Terriers need to get used to being handled also, but this can be done at home while being groomed and bathed, and the more it is done, the sooner they get used to it. The pet Yorkshire Terrier is just as versatile as a show Yorkshire Terrier and all of them enjoy the result of being groomed and looking beautiful.

Visiting the veterinary surgeon can sometimes be an ordeal for the Yorkshire Terrier as a puppy or adult, so it is important that you choose one that is familiar with and happy to handle a small dog. If your dog is used to being handled, he will find visits to the vet much less stressful.

EARLY LEAD TRAINING

Wearing a collar can be tricky initially, as most Yorkshire Terrier puppies, in common with other breeds, do not like anything around their necks. It is another gradual process for you to achieve, and encouragement and praise is necessary for your puppy to get used to this. Initially, he will pull and tug and scratch at the collar, but by wearing it for short periods and gradually increasing the time it is worn, success will eventually be achieved.

Walking on the lead is another exercise that requires time and patience. Yorkshire Terriers are quite strongwilled and often need firm handling. A young puppy pulling on the lead seems difficult, as he is so small, but co-operation follows eventually when he knows you mean to persist. It is important not to get angry; if tempers are getting frayed, it is wiser to stop. However, do not stop when the pup is 'winning'; only stop when you have achieved a victory, however small. A Yorkshire Terrier soon learns to know when you will be giving in to him, but also knows that praise is much more preferable. Eventually, your Yorkshire Terrier will be happy to walk on the lead and will walk proudly at your side; then you can take your puppy outside to learn about the outside world and meet other dogs.

If you are going to keep your Yorkie in full coat, he needs to become accustomed to daily grooming so that he relaxes and enjoys the attention.

THE BEST OF CARE

Chapter 5

When you take on a Yorkshire Terrier, you are responsible for all his needs for the duration of his life. You must give him the correct diet, care for his coat, provide preventative health care, and be aware of his general wellbeing so you can spot signs of trouble at an early stage.

PRINCIPLES OF FEEDING

The Yorkshire Terrier may be a small dog, but he still needs a balanced diet with all the nutrients to keep him healthy. Here is a brief outline of what is required in his diet.

FATS

Fats are an important part of a dog's diet. They have three main uses: firstly, they make the food palatable; secondly, they are a great energy provider; and thirdly, fats are a source of essential fatty acids. Like most nutrients, it is important to get the correct balance. Fats fed in moderation are essential; excess could lead to obesity, whereas a deficiency could result in skin disorders or reproductive problems.

PROTEINS

Protein is responsible for growth and development of muscle, and it also helps to defend the body against disease. Protein can be found in meat and offal. A puppy will require more protein than an adult: a puppy will need between 24 and 33 per cent whilst an adult will only require 10 to 14 per cent. Pregnant and lactating bitches will require extra to help produce milk and keep them strong and well.

CARBOHYDRATES

Carbohydrates, found in rice and pasta, can be mixed into the dog's food (in small quantities) and are very good for the Yorkie's coat, helping to keep it in good condition. Carbohydrates are a source of glucose, which gives the dog energy. However, it should only be fed in small amounts unless to a pregnant or nursing bitch.

VITAMINS AND MINERALS

The proprietary brands of dog food will all include the correct amount of vitamins and minerals needed to keep your dog healthy. Alternatively, you can buy vitamin tablets or powder from either your vet or pet shop.

- **Vitamin A** is essential for bone and muscle growth in puppies.
- **Vitamin B** helps to ensure normal growth in puppies and helps avoid convulsions and anaemia.
- **Vitamin D** is present in bitch's milk and dried milk for puppies and helps prevent

rickets, osteomalacia (bone softening) and milk fever in nursing bitches.

- **Vitamin E** is essential for breeding stock, both dogs and bitches. It can be found in wheat-germ meal; it is also good for the blood and coat condition. Cod-liver oil is another excellent source of vitamins A, D and E.

CHOOSING A DIET

Today, it is so easy to feed your Yorkshire Terrier properly, as the dog food manufacturers do all the hard work for you. There are different options to choose from, depending on what you find the most convenient and what suits your dog.

You need to find a well-balanced diet that will provide for all your Yorkshire Terrier's nutritional needs.

COMPLETE

There are two types of complete foods: wet and dry.

Wet: This is sold in plastic trays and generally consists of chicken or lamb with added brown rice and vegetables. Some have added salmon oil, seaweed, vitamins, minerals, glucosamine and chondroitin. A typical analysis would be:

- Protein 12 per cent
- Oil 8.0 per cent
- Fibre 1.6 per cent
- Ash 3.5 per cent
- Moisture 71 per cent
- Vitamin A 1750 iu/KG
- Vitamin D3 160 iu/KG
- Vitamin E 30iu/KG.

Dry: A dry complete diet will also contain all the nourishment your dog will require, from a growing puppy through to adulthood and veteran. A typical analysis would be:

- Fat: 18 per cent
- Protein: 28 per cent
- Carbohydrates: 37.8 per cent.

Yorkshire Terriers, being small dogs, have small stomachs, so they need a little more intake of protein. There is one manufacturer that makes a dry food especially for Yorkshire Terriers for when they are 10 months and over. I add some fresh meat to this – a little poached chicken or raw minced beef – as dogs enjoy the taste of meat and it makes their meals a little more interesting. The dried food range also has a product for the obese dog, which contains lower levels of protein and fat. Dried food varies in price a great deal; I would suggest that you buy the best you can afford.

CANNED

Another option is to use a canned food or the foil-topped food, which is made especially for small dogs. You will need to feed a small-bite mixer biscuit with the meat. This is one of the easiest ways to feed your dog and will fit in with a busy lifestyle. It is a perfectly suitable diet for a pet dog, though it is probably not as convenient as dry food, and, being wet and therefore made up in large part of water, it is not as 'nutrient dense' as dry food.

TYPES OF FOOD

A complete diet is is geared to lifestage feeding – giving your dog the nutrition he needs as he grows from puppy to adulthood and into old age.

Most dogs find canned food very appetising, but bear in mind that it has a high moisture content.

HOMEMADE

Some owners like to provide a homemade diet. You can buy fresh meat and cook it yourself or you can use minced beef or green tripe (only available at pet shops) and feed it raw. You will need to add biscuit meal or some dried food. If you are feeding fresh meat, it is a good idea to give your dog liver once a week, fried in a little butter and oil. Liver is an excellent form of vitamin B1, which is very good for the blood. I find that pig liver is the only type that does not result in diarrhoea.

There is another feeding method, which I know little about, so would suggest anyone interested should either buy a book or research on the internet: it is the Bones and Raw Food diet (BARF). It involves feeding raw meat, usually chicken wings, and raw vegetables, which have been pulped. Basically, this method mimics dogs in the wild living on raw meat and the stomachs of prey.

WATER

Fresh drinking water should be available at all times, regardless of diet, though it is particularly important if your Yorkie is fed a dry diet. Water makes up about 70 per cent of the adult dog's bodyweight, and therefore water forms the most important part of a dog's diet. The water bowl should be washed and re-filled daily.

TREATS

Treats, such as biscuits and chews, are appreciated, as they prevent boredom if you have to leave your Yorkie on his own for a while, and the process of gnawing and chewing also helps to keep the teeth clean.

Be careful of some of the thin hide chews. When chewed for a long time they have a tendency to go soft. I have known Yorkshire Terrier puppies to swallow a large piece of these chews, and they would have choked had no one been around to dislodge it.

DANGERS OF OBESITY

Yorkshire Terriers can sometimes be 'finicky' eaters. As a result, some uninformed owners can be reduced to feeding their dog whatever he will eat in order to ensure that he is at least taking in some food. While well intentioned, this is a misguided course of action. A dog fed a diet consisting largely of scraps of human food will be malnourished and may also become overweight if the diet is high in fat. Lack of exercise can also contribute to obesity. Unfortunately, because the Yorkshire Terrier is such a small dog, it is easy for him to become overweight if his diet and exercise regime are not well balanced.

Obesity causes many problems for dogs, not dissimilar to humans. Respiratory and joint problems are common, and a shortened life expectancy is the norm. Therefore, it is far better to establish a good diet and regular exercise as soon as possible, so that obesity never has to be faced.

To begin with, follow the diet sheet supplied by your puppy's breeder.

Most adults thrive on being fed twice a day.

FEEDING A PUPPY

A puppy usually goes to his new home at 8 to 10 weeks, and at this stage he will be having three meals a day. The breeder will usually give you a diet sheet recommending the type of food the puppies have been fed, and stipulating quantities. It is advisable to stick to this, at least for the first few weeks, so as not to upset the puppy's stomach. If you wish to change diet, introduce the new food gradually to avoid digestive upsets. When a puppy reaches six months his meals can be reduced to two a day, but the quantity of food should be increased so that the overall amounts remain the same.

FEEDING AN ADULT

When your Yorkshire Terrier is 12 months old, you can reduce his meals to one a day, but I prefer to feed two smaller meals so as not to overload the stomach. Some people prefer to free feed, leaving a dish of dried food down permanently so that the dog can snack all day. This works fine unless you have a greedy dog, where there is a danger of the dog becoming obese.

Yorkshire Terriers have a reputation for being a bit picky when it comes to food, though this does not apply to all Yorkies by any means. Sometimes a dog will be picky for a few days but soon recover his appetite.

Therefore, it is worth persevering for a few days before deciding that a certain food will always be rejected. A supplement containing vitamin B is a good appetite stimulant, which may also help.

GROOMING ROUTINES

The Yorkshire Terrier has a high-maintenance coat that will need regular attention. Of course, if you are showing your dog and keeping him in full coat, the workload steps up dramatically.

PUPPY GROOMING

It is essential that your puppy becomes used to being groomed from an early age so that he

THE YOKSHIRE TERRIER: PUPPY TO ADULT

The puppy coat needs little grooming, but it is important for a puppy to get used to brushing and combing. At this stage, the coat colour is black with tan markings.

This pup now has enough hair to take into a top-knot, although the body coat is still quite short. Note the blue colour is beginning to come through.

At 18 months, this Yorkshire Terrier is in the early stages of developing his full coat. The rich tan colour is now evident on the head furnishings.

accepts the attention. In fact, most Yorkshire Terriers enjoy being groomed, as they appreciate the quality one-on-one attention from their owner. If you buy the correct tools, it will help you groom your puppy effectively. You will need a steel comb with half-coarse teeth and half-fine teeth, plus a good-quality pure bristle brush, such as those manufactured by Mason Pearson or Kent.

To get your puppy used to being handled and groomed, it is best to start as soon as he has settled in his new home. You will need to place a rubber mat on a table to prevent him from slipping, and it is also important

to have one hand on the puppy at all times to prevent him from jumping and injuring himself.

Start with the face, and gently comb the puppy all over, paying particular attention to his chest, legs and under carriage. A good tip is to have a small water spray bottle at your side. If you find a small knot, you can spray water on it, which will help when you comb it out. You will find it much easier to comb a damp coat. When the coat is combed through and knot-free, you can brush it and make it shine. When you are grooming, check the rear end, and clean if necessary. This job should be done on a daily basis.

This is also a good time to check your puppy's nails for trimming. Be very careful not to cut the nails too short, as this could damage the quick and result in bleeding. These cuts always look worse than they are, as they produce a lot of blood, which can be scary for both dog and owner alike. The first time your dog needs his nails trimmed, it is a good idea to get your vet to do it. He or she can show you what to do so that you are ready for the next time.

You should also incorporate brushing your dog's teeth into your grooming routine. You can buy very good meat-flavoured doggie toothpastes. Use either a

BATHING A PUPPY

You can bath your puppy as often as you wish, but every three to four weeks is usual. Bathing your puppy should be an enjoyable process and everything you will need should be to hand, in order to help things run smoothly.

For a puppy's first bath, the kitchen sink is the easiest place. Put a bowl with lukewarm water on the draining board and about three or four inches of lukewarm water in the sink, unless you have a shower attachment for the taps, which will make life much easier. If not, you will need a small jug to wet and rinse the puppy. You will also need shampoo and a baby 'no tears' shampoo for the face, as well as conditioner and a soft towel. Have your hairdryer plugged in close to the grooming table, making sure you have rubber mat in place.

- Place the puppy in the sink, keeping hold of him with one hand at all times. With your free hand, gently wet the puppy all over.
- Apply a little shampoo on the body, and massage it in with your fingers. Next apply shampoo to the legs and massage it in.
- Change to the baby shampoo and, very carefully, wash his face and head.
- Rinse the coat thoroughly.
- Now is the time to put on a small amount of conditioner. You will need to rinse thoroughly again, making sure that none is left in the coat.
- Wrap your puppy in a towel and take him to the table to be dried.
- Towel-dry him first, then, while he is still wet, comb him through, starting with the coarse side of the comb and finishing with the fine side.

Now you are all set to switch on your hair dryer; using a medium heat, gently brush and dry him completely.

baby toothbrush or a special rubber-ribbed thimble especially designed for the purpose (these fit on your finger so you use your finger to clean the teeth). The adult teeth usually come through when the puppy is between five and six months of age. By then, teeth brushing will hopefully be routine, so that your Yorkie can keep a great set of teeth into his dotage.

This grooming procedure should be repeated two or three times a week. Each session needs to last only about 10 minutes. If a puppy resists, stop and try again a little later. Try giving a treat to reward co-operation, even if the session lasts just two minutes. You can build on a positive experience until your puppy is standing still for the required 10 minutes. When your puppy is five or six months, he will require daily attention to keep his hair clean and free from knots.

GROOMING FOR SHOW

If you decide to show your Yorkshire Terrier, you are committed to a lot of hard work in order to groom and cultivate the coat, but if you are dedicated, your hard work will pay off and you will end up with a glamorous dog that is a joy to behold. Theo Marples, the founder and editor of the weekly newspaper *Our Dogs*, wrote in his book, *Show Dogs*: The Yorkshire Terrier is still the prettiest and most elegant

The work that goes into keeping a dog in full coat is formidable.

morsel of toy dog flesh on the British show bench.

Les Griffiths, of the world famous Beechrise affix, wrote the following, which I hope will help you to understand this most beautiful breed.

"What makes the Yorkie unique?... His coat, of course!"

Why is this Toy Terrier unique? Was it clever breeding or did it just happen by chance? No one will ever know, so many theories have been put forward. I have often wondered why the early breeders set the standard so high. Fifty per cent of the one hundred points allocated to make the perfect Yorkshire Terrier are given to coat, colours, wealth, length, and texture of coat.

Why do I say the breed is unique? What other Breed Standard demands metallic colours, the head, the topknot of hair on the head, the fall and moustache?

The colour on the legs and feet remind me of a new gold sovereign; the depth of colour at the roots of the hair gets paler towards the ends. The Standard also says free from black or sooty type hair intermingling with the golden tan.

The dark steel body coat is often quoted as being like a polished gun barrel. There can be many differences of opinion as to the correct shade of blue but one thing is definite: the colour should be even right through.

The golden tan ends at the back of the skull, the steel blue starts where

71

the neck begins. The division between the two colours should be definite with no intermingling.

The colour on the tail should be darker than the body. The golden tan on the legs should not extend and intermingle with the body coat – this is known as running colours.

The Yorkie is a single-coated dog. Very similar in texture to human hair, they do not shed coat periodically like other dogs; the result is that from puppy stage to adult dog the hair grows longer and longer. This can be helped by care and cultivation. The correct hair is like silk. Each single hair if magnified for inspection can be seen to be individual. True silk is cool to the touch.

From a very early age the hair on top of the skull is tied in a topknot; by doing this it can become very long indeed. The fall comes from each side of the head, the hair is parted down the centre from nose to eye, to fall each side of the jaws. This is the moustache. The hair from the nape of the neck is parted down the centre of the back to the tail set, laying down quite straight each side of the body. This can be encouraged to grow right down to the floor length with the right care.

My wife and I have tried many coat oils and conditioners over the years but have always gone back to plain oils, almond oil.

If you want Yorkies with good coats, first and foremost breed for it. Select a sire and dam with qualities you are looking for. Studying pedigrees is a good way but never forget one important thing: like begets like. Like mother like daughter, like father like son and vice versa.

What more can one say except that careful grooming, cleanliness, good diet and a healthy dog all contribute to a healthy coat.

A top-quality Yorkshire Terrier coat is something that must be bred for.

A pure bristle brush is essential for grooming a dog in full coat.

You will need a comb with both coarse and fine teeth.

GROOMING EQUIPMENT

The following items are for everyday grooming:

- A comb with coarse and fine teeth
- Hairdressing scissors
- Almond oil or Vitapoint (or some other preparation that you prefer)
- A natural bristle brush (kept solely for oiling the coat)
- Acid-free tissue paper cut into strips 17cm long and 7cm wide (alternatively, you could buy the coloured tissue already cut, on sale at dog shows, and rubber bands to keep these in place). These are for tying up the dog's coat, which is known as crackering.
- A pair of nail cutters
- A rubber mat to stand the dog on while grooming
- A toothbrush (either for dogs or babies) with doggie toothpaste
- A tangle remover mixed with water in a spray bottle
- Boots for the back feet, made out of soft T-shirt materials or tubular finger bandage held in place with a piece of surgical tape.

For the show ring you will need the following additions:

- A comb with coarse and fine teeth
- A pure bristle brush with white long bristles (scour antique fairs and car-boot sales for this item)
- A small water spray
- Small rubber bands and a red bow for the topknot
- A wooden carrying box and red cover to stand your dog on in the show ring
- A fold-up grooming table and, of course, food and water for your dog

GETTING STARTED

Practise standing your puppy on the grooming table just for a few minutes, two or three times a week. He will need his feet trimming round to make them look small and neat. The top third of the hair from his ears will need to be around the outer edge to the shape of his ears so that the ears look neat and V-shaped. This is also a good time to get your puppy used to wearing little boots on his back feet. These prevent the dog from knotting his coat when scratching, which can cause a lot of damage, especially when he is old enough to have his coat crackered. The boots should be changed daily as part of his grooming routine.

This is the time to introduce your puppy to having a cracker in his topknot. Make sure you have a piece of the tissue paper and a rubber band at the ready, and then follow this procedure:

- Fold the tissue paper in half, then fold the top half over half an inch widthways and then three times lengthways. Now your cracker is ready.

- With the comb take a line from the ear to the corner of the eye on both sides. Then take a straight line at the back of the head from ear to ear.
- Comb the hair upwards and hold it in your left hand while putting the paper at the back in the middle with the folded-over edge next to the head. Then fold each of the outside thirds over the hair.
- Next double the paper over forwards once, then backwards once.
- Now put a band on to hold it in place, taking care not to have it too tight. If it is uncomfortable, he will rub his head.
- It may take a puppy a week or so to get used to wearing the cracker. To begin with, some Yorkshire Terriers will try to rub them on furniture or try to pull them out.

WRAPPING THE COAT

When your Yorkie reaches 12 months you can start to wrap all the coat. I would never tie the coat up before this time because I like my dogs to enjoy their puppyhood. It is also worth bearing in mind that if you wrap too early, you can do more harm than good, as a youngster is sure to rub, trying to get the papers out. Every groomer has his or her own methods, but this is the method I use:

- Pour a little almond oil into a saucer and, with your bristle

brush apply the oil to the coat, paying particular attention to the ends of the hair to keep it supple.

- Start by putting a small cracker on either side of the nose, making sure the hair is only taken from above the mouth to allow the dog to open his mouth.
- Then put another cracker under the chin, and one on either side of the cheeks.
- When you have completed the head, turn your dog away from you. Put a cracker underneath his tail in the bottom third. The top part of the tail will need trimming almost like a fan to make it look tidy.
- Make a straight parting down the neck and back with the comb. Turn the dog sideways and put four crackers down either side of his body, making sure the dog has freedom of movement.
- Put a cracker on the hind leg, next one up to the end of his ribs, then the rib area and then the shoulder. In other words, follow the dog's natural movement. Then put a cracker in the neck.
- Turn the dog around and repeat the procedure on the other side, but please make sure that he has freedom of movement.
- Now only one left to go, and that is the chest.

Sometimes the dog (or his kennel mates) pull the crackers from the body. If this happens, you will need to purchase a silk

coat to protect the crackers. There are some good Yorkshire Terrier grooming videos and DVDs available, as you might find it easier to watch the procedure or perhaps your puppy's breeder will help you. The process of wrapping the coat must be carried out every day. It is easier to comb the crackers out individually and then wrap them up again rather than taking them all out together.

BATHING THE SHOW COAT

Bathing the show coat takes a lot of time and care, so make sure you never have to work against the clock. It is easier to bathe an adult dog in the bath with a shower spray, making sure you have a rubber bath mat to prevent the dog slipping.

- Remove all the crackers and brush the coat out.
- Wet the coat all over and shampoo two or three times, making sure that all the oil is removed, rinsing after each shampoo.
- Apply conditioner, making sure it reaches the ends of the coat, and then rinse thoroughly to ensure that there are no residues of shampoo or conditioner.
- Squeeze the excess water from the hair, making sure you keep one hand on the dog all the time to prevent him from shaking and wetting you through.
- Wrap him in a towel and transport him to the grooming table where you should have

WRAPPING THE COAT

This is a lengthy process but it protects the long hair and allows the show dog to move about with relative freedom. The coat is divided into small sections, and then wrapped in individual 'packets' of tissue paper. This process is also known as 'crackering' the coat.

Place the hair in the centre of the tissue paper and then fold both sides.

The hair is now enclosed in tissue paper and is ready to be folded upwards.

The tissue paper is folded in half...

....then in quarters.

The tissue paper 'packet' is the right size.

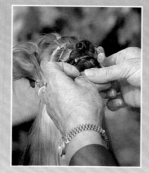

It can now be secured with a rubber band.

The head furnishings will need to be protected with five crackers: two on either side of the head, one for the top-knot and one for the hair on the chin.

The body hair and tail is also put into crackers. The hair around the feet is protected with boots.

your hairdryer plugged in close by.

- Start by gently squeezing the coat with the towel. Do not rub, as this will knot the coat.
- It would be best if you had a dryer that leaves both hands free, but if not, don't worry. As you are drying the dog, brush the coat continually to keep it straight until it is completely dry. When you are sure that the dog is dry and

free from any wrinkles or waves, use a small rubber band to put his hair in a topknot and put in the customary red bow. Now you are all set for the show.

GROOMING THE PET YORKIE

There are many ways to keep the pet Yorkie, depending on the time you have available for coat care. You can keep the hair to its

natural length by regular brushing and combing. The ears and feet will need trimming, and you will have to bath your Yorkie every couple of weeks, using a good shampoo and conditioner. An anti-tangle spray is also a good aid for keeping the coat tangle-free. A pet Yorkie's coat will not grow to floor length if it is not tied up like the show dog coat.

There are lots of different types of haircuts for the person with no time for grooming. If you are handy with a pair of scissors, you could trim the coat yourself. The other option is to take your Yorkie for a visit to the grooming parlour where the groomer can advise you of the various haircuts and can make grooming at home minimal, which will be much easier for a busy household. The short haircut keeps the dog cleaner in winter, as the long coat gathers leaves and twigs and is very often wet.

Bathing the pet Yorkshire Terrier is, of course, much easier than the show Yorkie. He will still require careful handling, of course, but one or two shampoos with a good-quality dog shampoo and a little conditioner will be sufficient, as there's no oil in the coat. You can also towel-dry, giving a little rub, as the hair will not tangle, and finish off with the hairdryer, brushing as you dry.

NAILS

Nails should be checked regularly; if your dog doesn't exercise on hard ground, the nails will grow long and need trimming. If you are cutting

There are a number of ways to trim a pet Yorkie, depending on how much coat you want to keep.

THE PET YORKIE

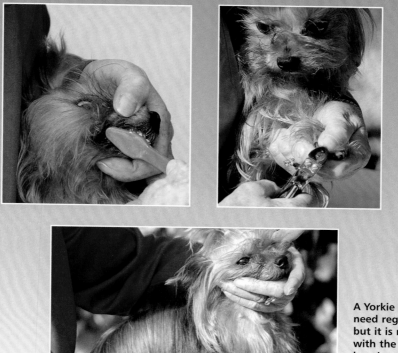

Regular teeth cleaning will prevent the build-up of plaque.

Nails will need to be trimmed, taking care not to cut into the quick.

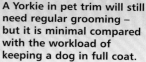

A Yorkie in pet trim will still need regular grooming – but it is minimal compared with the workload of keeping a dog in full coat.

them yourself, just cut the end that bends round, taking care not to cut into the quick. If you are nervous or unsure, it would be advisable to leave it to a vet or a groomer.

TEETH
It is important to brush your dog's teeth regularly, and most enjoy the meat-flavoured toothpaste. Sometimes you have

to crack the plaque off the teeth with a descaler or, if it gets too bad, you might have to ask your vet to do a thorough cleaning under anaesthetic.

EARS
The Yorkshire Terrier's ears need regular checking for wax and ear mites. Hair growing in the ear canal should be carefully plucked out with tweezers. A

little canker powder put in the ear first will make this procedure much easier.

EYES
The Yorkie's eyes will require cleaning as part of your daily grooming routine. A little dry matter can be combed away, but a bigger deposit will require bathing with warm water and cotton wool.

Obviously a Yorkshire Terrier in full coat cannot enjoy the complete freedom of a Yorkie in pet trim, but he still needs to be kept active and will enjoy the mental stimulation of playing games.

EXERCISING YORKIES

During the first year of your puppy's life, his joints and bones are very delicate. He needs to play and have walks, but walking too far can affect his joints in later life. You will also need to make sure your puppy doesn't jump on or off furniture, as their limbs can be so easily broken. A stair gate will prevent a puppy going upstairs (and falling downstairs).

The adult Yorkie will need plenty of daily exercise to keep fit, maintain muscle tone and also to keep him mentally stimulated. The amount of exercise to give depends on the individual dog. Some will get sufficient exercise from playing in the garden (especially if there is more than one dog) plus just a short walk; others like to go for long walks but they are not essential.

Most Yorkshire Terriers like toys, so, for the single dog with an owner that does not have much time for walking, games can be played with the toys, indoors or out, retrieving or playing hide-and-seek. Some Yorkies can even find a named toy, no matter how carefully it is hidden. Another fun way of exercising both mind and body is to train in agility where dogs compete at speed on an obstacle course, going through tunnels and slaloms, over jumps, and so on. It is very rewarding but will require regular training and practice. If you are interested in taking up this sport, it would be advisable to do a basic training course first, as the dogs have to work off the lead. When my children were young they used to erect small hurdles in the garden, and the dogs and children used to have great fun playing and keeping fit.

CARING FOR THE OLDER DOG

Yorkshire Terriers usually live to a good age, around 15 years on average, although I have known some live to their early 20s. My personal oldest was 18. Yorkies, like most Toy breeds, have usually lost all their teeth by the time they are 10 and are usually seen with their tongue hanging out, as they haven't any teeth to hold it in place. This is why it is so important to establish good dental care early on, so that your Yorkie can keep his teeth for as long as possible. You may need to change your Yorkie's diet so that he can eat without teeth, and his nutritional needs will alter as he ages anyway. There are a lot of senior dog foods on the market for dogs aged seven and over, and your vet can advise you further.

Your Yorkie's grooming needs will also change with his advancing years. I think the kindest solution is to cut the hair short to make brushing and combing less time-consuming, but I would still recommend regular bathing. Even if you keep the coat very short, it is important to spend some time grooming so that you stimulate the skin, and, most importantly, continue to reinforce the bond between dog and owner that is established through grooming.

LETTING GO

In your Yorkie's last years you should keep him warm and give him lots of love. You may come down one morning and find that he has passed peacefully in his sleep. More likely, you will reach a time where you can see he is no longer enjoying life. Do not let him suffer. If the case arises where your vet recommends euthanasia, however difficult it is for you, remember that it is the kindest act you can do for your dog. It gives you a chance to say goodbye properly, while cradling your Yorkie so that he is not alone. In some cases, the vet may even come to the house so that your beloved pet can pass in familiar surroundings.

Coping with the loss of a dog that has been a much-loved family member for so many years can be very difficult. The grief can be as bad as losing a member of the human family. There are bereavement groups that can help you to deal with the loss of a pet, as well as several books about the subject. Hold on to the fact that, in time, the grief will fade and you will be left with the happy memories of your wonderful Yorkie instead.

The older Yorkshire Terrier deserves special consideration.

TRAINING & SOCIALISATION

Chapter 6

When you decided to bring a Yorkshire Terrier into your life, you probably had dreams of how it was going to be – enjoying the companionship of a loyal, devoted, little dog, who has the added bonus of being one of the most glamorous breeds in the pedigree world.

There is no doubt that a Yorkshire Terrier will fulfil this role, but like anything that is worth having, you must be prepared to put in the work. A Yorkie, regardless of whether he is a puppy or an adult, does not come ready trained, understanding exactly what you want and fitting perfectly into your lifestyle. He has to learn his place in your family and he must discover what is acceptable behaviour.

We have a great starting point in that the breed has an outstanding temperament. The Yorkshire Terrier is quick-witted, intelligent and eager to please, and, perhaps most important of all, his greatest desire is to be with his beloved human family.

THE FAMILY PACK

Dogs have been domesticated for some 14,000 years, but luckily for us, they have inherited and retained behaviour from their distant ancestor – the wolf. A Yorkie may never have lived in the wild, but he is born with the survival skills and the mentality of a meat-eating predator who hunts in a pack. A wolf living in a pack owes its existence to mutual co-operation and an acceptance of a hierarchy, as this ensures both food and protection. A domesticated dog living in a family pack has exactly the same outlook. He wants food, companionship, and leadership – and it is your job to provide for these needs.

YOUR ROLE

Theories about dog behaviour and methods of training go in and out of fashion, but in reality, nothing has changed from the day when wolves ventured in from the wild to join the family circle. The wolf (and equally the dog) accepts a subservient place in the family pack in return for food and protection. In a dog's eyes, you are his leader and he relies on you to make all the important decisions. This does not mean that you have to act like a dictator or a bully. You are accepted as a leader, without argument, as long as you have the right credentials.

The first part of the job is easy. You are the provider and you are therefore respected because you supply food. In a Yorkshire Terrier's eyes, you must be the ultimate hunter, because a day never goes by when you cannot find food. The second part of the leader's job description is straightforward, but for some reason we find it hard to achieve. In order for a dog to accept his place in the family pack, he must respect his leader as the decision-maker. A low-ranking pack animal does not question authority; he is perfectly happy to see someone else shoulder the responsibility. Problems will only arise if you cut a poor figure as leader and the dog feels he should mount a challenge for the top-ranking role.

HOW TO BE A GOOD LEADER

There are a number of guidelines to follow to establish yourself in the role of leader in a way that your Yorkshire Terrier understands and respects. If you have a puppy, you may think you don't have to take this on board for a few months – or you may think that a small dog does not need to be trained – but that would be a big mistake. With a Yorkshire Terrier it is absolutely essential to start as you mean to go on and establish your credentials as leader. The Yorkie may be small in stature, but he is big on self-esteem and will be quick to take advantage. The behaviour he learns as a puppy will continue throughout his adult life, which means that undesirable behaviour can be very difficult to rectify.

When your Yorkshire Terrier first arrives in his new home, follow these guidelines:

- **Keep it simple:** Decide on the rules you want your Yorkie to obey and always make it 100 per cent clear what is acceptable, and what is unacceptable, behaviour.

- **Be consistent:** If you are not consistent about enforcing rules, how can you expect your Yorkshire Terrier to take you seriously? There is nothing worse than allowing your Yorkie to jump on the sofa one moment and then scolding him the next time he does it because he is wet or muddy. As far as the dog is concerned, he may as well try it on because he cannot predict your reaction. Bear in mind, inconsistency leads to insecurity.

- **Get your timing right:** If you are rewarding your Yorkshire Terrier and equally if you are reprimanding him, you must respond within one to two seconds, otherwise the dog will not link his behaviour with your reaction (see page 87).

- **Read your dog's body language:** Find out how to read body language and facial expressions (see page 84) so that you understand your Yorkie's feelings and intentions.

- **Be aware of your own body language:** You can also help your dog to learn by using your body language to communicate with him. For example, if you want your dog to come to you, open your arms out and look inviting. If you want your dog to stay, use a hand signal (palm flat, facing the dog) so you are effectively 'blocking' his advance.

Do you have what it takes to be a firm, fair and consistent leader?

- **Tone of voice:** Dogs do not speak English; they learn by associating a word with the required action. However, they are very receptive to tone of voice, so you can use your voice to praise him or to correct undesirable behaviour. If you are pleased with your Yorkshire Terrier, praise him to the skies in a warm, happy voice. If you want to stop him raiding the bin, use a deep, stern voice when you say "No".

- **Give one command only:** If you keep repeating a command, or keep changing it, your Yorkie will think you are babbling and will probably ignore you. If you are not careful, he will get into the habit of ignoring you when it suits him – and in no time, you have a dog that does not respect you. So, if your Yorkshire Terrier does not respond the first time you ask, make it simple by using a treat to lure him into position and then you can reward him for a correct response.

- **Daily reminders:** A Yorkshire Terrier is clever enough to turn situations to his own advantage, and you may find that your dog tries to push his luck – particularly during adolescence when he may be testing the boundaries (see page 97). Rather than coming down on him like a ton of bricks when he does something wrong, try to prevent bad manners by daily reminders of good manners.

For example:

i.   Do not let your Yorkshire Terrier barge ahead of you when you are going through a door.

ii. Do not let him leap out of the car the moment you open the door (which could be potentially lethal, as well as being disrespectful).

iii. Do not let him eat from your hand when you are at the table.

iv. Do not let him 'win' a toy at the end of a play session and then make off with it. You 'own' his toys and you 'allow' him to play with them. Your Yorkshire Terrier must learn to give up a toy when you ask.

UNDERSTANDING YOUR YORKSHIRE TERRIER

Body language is an important means of communication between dogs, which they use to make friends, to assert status and to avoid conflict. It is important to get on your dog's wavelength by understanding his body language and reading his facial expressions. If you own a Yorkshire Terrier, it is also important that you 'read' other dogs' body language. A Yorkshire Terrier is generally very friendly with other dogs, and he is completely fearless – no matter the size of the other dog. This can lead to misunderstanding, as the bigger dog may become worried by the Yorkie's exuberance and not know how to react to such a small dog. For this

Stick to the house rules at all times, so your Yorkie understands what is acceptable behaviour.

MEETING AND GREETING

You can learn a lot about dog body language if you watch dogs meeting and greeting.

These puppies are worried about meeting a bigger dog and appear apprehensive. Their body language is submissive with ears back and appeasing expressions.

The Labrador is calm and quiet, showing that he does not pose a threat.

The pup now feels confident enough to start a game.

For some Yorkies, a food treat is a reward worth working for.

Other dogs are motivated by toys.

reason, you should always be vigilant when your Yorkshire Terrier is in a situation where he might meet strange dogs.

When you are observing dogs meeting and greeting, look for the following signs:

- A positive body posture and a wagging tail indicate a happy, confident dog.
- A crouched body posture with ears back and tail down show that a dog is being submissive. A dog may do this when he is being told off or if a more assertive dog approaches him.
- A bold dog will stand tall, looking strong and alert. His ears will be forward and his tail will be held high.
- A dog who raises his hackles (lifting the fur along his topline) is trying to look as scary as possible.

- A playful dog will go down on his front legs while standing on his hind legs in a bow position. This friendly invitation says: "I'm no threat, let's play."
- A nervous dog will often show aggressive behaviour as a means of self-protection. If threatened, this dog will lower his head and flatten his ears. The corners of his mouth may be drawn back and he may bark or whine.

GIVING REWARDS

Why should your Yorkshire Terrier do as you ask? If you follow the guidelines given above, your Yorkie should respect your authority, but what about the time when he is playing with a new doggy friend or has found a really enticing scent? The answer is that you must always be the

most interesting, the most attractive and the most irresistible person in your Yorkshire Terrier's eyes. It would be nice to think that you could achieve this by personality alone, but most of us need a little extra help. You need to find out what is the biggest reward for your dog. A Yorkshire Terrier will work for food treats, but many select a toy as a special favourite, and a game with this is seen as the biggest reward. But whatever reward you use, make sure it is something that your dog really wants.

When you are teaching a dog a new exercise, you should reward your Yorkie frequently. When he knows the exercise or command, reward him randomly so that he keeps on responding to you in a positive manner.

If your Yorkshire Terrier does

something extra special – like leaving an enticing scent to come when you call him – make sure he really knows how pleased you are by giving him a handful of treats or having an extra long game with his favourite toy. If your Yorkie gets a bonanza reward, he is more likely to come back on future occasions because you have proved to be even more rewarding than his previous activity.

TOP TREATS
Some trainers grade treats depending on what they are asking the dog to do. A dog may get a low-grade treat (such as a piece of dry food) to reward good behaviour on a random basis, such as sitting when you open a door or allowing you to examine his teeth. High-grade treats (which may be cooked liver, sausage or cheese) may be reserved for training new exercises, or for use in the park when you want a really good recall, for example.

Whatever type of treat you use, you should remember to subtract it from your Yorkshire Terrier's daily food ration. Yorkies are prone to obesity, particularly if they do not get a lot of exercise. Fat dogs are lethargic, prone to health problems and will almost certainly have a shorter life expectancy, so reward your Yorkie, but always keep a check on his figure!

HOW DO DOGS LEARN?
It is not difficult to get inside your Yorkshire Terrier's head and understand how he learns, as it is not dissimilar to the way we learn. Dogs learn by conditioning: they find out that specific behaviours produce specific consequences. This is

BE POSITIVE!

The most effective method of training dogs is to use their ability to learn by consequence and to teach that the behaviour you want produces a good consequence. For example, if you ask your Yorkshire to "Sit" and reward him with a treat, he will learn that it is worth his while to sit on command because it will lead to a reward. He is far more likely to repeat the behaviour, and the behaviour will become stronger, because it results in a positive outcome. This method of training is known as positive reinforcement and it generally leads to a happy, co-operative dog that is willing to work and a handler who has fun training their dog.

The opposite approach is negative reinforcement. This is far less effective and often results in a poor relationship between dog and owner.

In this method of training, you ask your Yorkie to "Sit" and if he does not respond, you deliver a sharp yank on the training collar or push his rear to the ground. The dog learns that not responding to your command has a bad consequence and he may be less likely to ignore you in the future. However, it may well have a bad consequence for you, too. A dog that is treated in this way may associate harsh handling with the handler and become aggressive or fearful. Instead of establishing a pattern of willing co-operation, you are establishing a relationship built on coercion.

known as operant conditioning or consequence learning. Consequences have to be immediate or clearly linked to the behaviour, as a dog sees the world in terms of action and result. Dogs will quickly learn if an action has a bad consequence or a good consequence.

Dogs also learn by association. This is known as classical conditioning or association learning. It is the type of learning made famous by Pavlov's experiment with dogs. Pavlov presented dogs with food and measured their salivary response (how much they drooled). Then he rang a bell just before presenting the food. At first, the dogs did not salivate until the food was presented. But after a while they learnt that the sound of the bell meant that food was coming and so they salivated when they heard the bell. A dog needs to learn the association in order for it to have any meaning. For example, a dog that has never seen a lead before will be completely indifferent to it. A dog that has learnt that a lead means he is going for a walk will get excited the second he sees the lead; he has learnt to associate a lead with a walk.

GETTING STARTED

As you train your Yorkshire Terrier you will develop your own techniques as you get to know what motivates him. You may decide to get involved with clicker training or you may prefer to go for a simple command-and-reward formula. It does not matter what form of training you use, as long as it is based on positive, reward-based methods.

There are a few important guidelines to bear in mind when you are training your Yorkshire Terrier:

• Find a training area that is free

A dog learns by linking an action with a consequence.

THE CLICKER REVOLUTION

Karen Pryor pioneered the technique of clicker training when she was working with dolphins. It is very much a continuation of Pavlov's work and makes full use of association learning. Karen wanted to mark 'correct' behaviour at the precise moment it happened. She found it was impossible to toss a fish to a dolphin when it was in mid-air, when she wanted to reward it. Her aim was to establish a conditioned response so the dolphin knew that it had performed correctly and a reward would follow.

The solution was the clicker: a small matchbox-shaped training aid, with a metal tongue that makes a click when it is pressed. To begin with, the dolphin had to learn that a click meant that food was coming. The dolphin then learnt that it must 'earn' a click in order to get a reward. Clicker training has been used with many different animals, most particularly with dogs, and it has proved hugely successful. It is a great aid for pet owners and is also widely used by professional trainers who teach highly specialised skills.

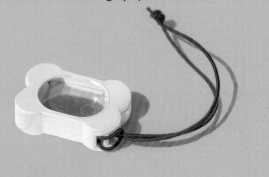

from distractions, particularly when you are just starting out. This applies to all breeds, but most particularly to the Yorkshire Terrier. This is a breed that is easily distracted, and his attention will wander unless you work at keeping him focused. For this reason, it may be easier to train him indoors to begin with.

- Keep training sessions short, especially with young puppies that have very short attention spans.
- Do not train if you are in a bad mood or if you are on a tight schedule – the training session will be doomed to failure.
- If you are using a toy as a reward, make sure it is only available when you are training. In this way it has an added value for your Yorkshire Terrier.
- If you are using food treats, make sure they are bite-size and easy to swallow; you don't want to hang about while your Yorkie chews on his treat.
- Do not attempt to train your Yorkshire Terrier after he has eaten, or soon after returning from exercise. He will either be too full up to care about food treats or too tired to concentrate.
- When you are training, move around your allocated area so that your dog does not think that an exercise can only be performed in one place.
- If your Yorkie is finding an exercise difficult, try not to get frustrated. Go back a step and praise him for his effort. You will probably find he is more successful when you try again at the next training session.
- If a training session is not going well – either because you are in the wrong frame of mind

or the dog is not focusing – ask your Yorkshire Terrier to do something you know he can do (such as a trick he enjoys performing), and then you can reward him with a food treat or a play with his favourite toy, ending the session on a happy, positive note.

• Keep it fun. The Yorkshire Terrier is a very bright little dog and will quickly become bored if a training session becomes dull ands repetitive. Intersperse exercise with games and make sure you always end on a high, with your Yorkie wanting more, rather than making him sour by asking too much from him.

In the exercises that follow, clicker training is introduced and followed, but all the exercises will work without the use of a clicker.

INTRODUCING A CLICKER

This is dead easy, and the intelligent Yorkshire Terrier will learn about the clicker in record time! It can be combined with attention training, which is a very useful tool and can be used on many different occasions.

• Prepare some treats and go to an area that is free from distractions. Allow your Yorkie to wander and when he stops to look at you, click and reward by throwing him a treat. This means he will not crowd you, but will go looking for the treat. Repeat a couple of times. If your Yorkshire Terrier is very easily distracted, you may need to start this exercise with the dog on a lead.

• After a few clicks, your Yorkie will understand that if he hears a click, he will get a treat. He must now learn that he must 'earn' a click. This time, when your Yorkshire Terrier looks at you, wait a little longer before clicking and then reward him. If he is on a lead but responding well, try him off the lead.

• When your Yorkie is working for a click and giving you his attention, you can introduce a cue or command word, such as "Watch". Repeat a few times, using the cue. You now have a Yorkshire Terrier that understands the clicker and will give you his attention when you ask him to "Watch".

It will not take long before your Yorkie learns that a click means a reward will follow.

The Sit is easy to teach and can be applied in a wide variety of situations.

This Yorkie is being lured into the Down using a toy.

TRAINING EXERCISES

THE SIT

This is the easiest exercise to teach, so it is rewarding for both you and your Yorkie.

- Choose a tasty treat and hold it just above your puppy's nose. As he looks up at the treat, he will naturally go into the 'Sit'. As soon as he is in position, reward him.
- Repeat the exercise and when your pup understands what you want, introduce the "Sit" command.
- You can practise the Sit exercise at mealtimes by holding out the bowl and waiting for your dog to sit. Most Yorkies learn this one very quickly!

THE DOWN

Work hard at this exercise because a reliable 'Down' is useful in many different situations, and an instant 'Down' can be a lifesaver. You may think there is little point in teaching a tiny Toy dog to go into the Down position. But, in fact, most dogs feel more secure in the Down, and are more likely to remain in position when you teach the Stay exercise (see page 93).

- You can start with your dog in a 'Sit', or it is just as effective to teach it when the dog is standing. Hold a treat just below your puppy's nose and slowly lower it towards the ground. The treat acts as a lure and your puppy will follow it, first going down on his forequarters and then bringing his hindquarters down as he tries to get the treat.
- Make sure you close your fist around the treat and only reward your puppy with the treat when he is in the correct position. If your puppy is reluctant to go 'Down', you can apply gentle pressure on his shoulders to encourage him to go into the correct position.
- When your puppy is following the treat and going into position, introduce a verbal command.
- Build up this exercise over a period of time, each time waiting a little longer before

Make yourself sound exciting so your Yorkie wants to come to you.

giving the reward, so the puppy learns to stay in the 'Down' position.

THE RECALL

It is never too soon to begin teaching your Yorkshire Terrier the recall. This is a breed with strong scenting abilities and a lively curiosity. He is also completely fearless, and will rarely shy away from new situations. These are all plus points when you have a dog that is under control, but a dog who pleases himself and fails to respond to the recall can easily end up in trouble. As we have noted, the Yorkshire Terrier is generally happy to meet all dogs – regardless of their size – but there may be times when you need to

call your dog away for his own safety, if play is getting too rough, or the other dog is become worried.

Hopefully, the breeder will have already started recall training by calling the puppies in from outside and rewarding them with some treats scattered on the floor. But even if this has not been the case, you will find that a puppy arriving in his new home is highly responsive. His chief desire is to follow you and be with you. Capitalise on this from day one by getting your pup's attention and calling him to you in a bright, excited tone of voice.

• Practise in the garden. When your puppy is busy exploring, get his attention by calling his

name. As he runs towards you, introduce the verbal command "Come". Make sure you sound happy and exciting, so your puppy wants to come to you. When he responds, give him lots of praise.

• If your puppy is slow to respond, try running away a few paces, or jumping up and down. It doesn't matter how silly you look, the key issue is to get your puppy's attention and then make yourself irresistible!

• In a dog's mind, coming when called should be regarded as the best fun because he knows he is always going to be rewarded. Never make the mistake of telling your dog off,

SECRET WEAPON

You can build up a strong recall by using another form of association learning. Buy a whistle and when you are giving your Yorkshire Terrier his food, peep on the whistle. You can choose the type of signal you want to give: two short peeps or one long whistle, for example. Within a matter of days, your dog will learn that the sound of the whistle means that food is coming.

Now transfer the lesson outside. Arm yourself with some tasty treats and the whistle. Allow your Yorkie to run free in the garden, and, after a couple of minutes, use the whistle. The dog has already learnt to associate the whistle with food, so he will come towards you. Immediately

reward him with a treat and lots of praise. Repeat the lesson a few times in the garden, so you are confident that your dog is responding before trying it in the park. Make sure you always have some treats in your pocket when you go for a walk and your dog will quickly learn how rewarding it is to come to you.

no matter how slow he is to respond, as you will undo all your previous hard work.

- When you call your Yorkshire Terrier to you, make sure he comes up close enough to be touched. He must understand that "Come" means that he should come right up to you, otherwise he will think that he can approach and then veer off when it suits him.
- When you are free running your dog, make sure you have his favourite toy or a pocket full of treats so you can reward him at intervals throughout the walk when you call him to you. Do not allow your dog to free run and only call him back at

the end of the walk to clip on his lead. An intelligent Yorkshire Terrier will soon realise that the recall means the end of his walk and the end of fun – so who can blame him for not wanting to come back?

TRAINING LINE

This is the equivalent of a very long lead, which you can buy at a pet store, or you can make your own with a length of rope. The training line is attached to your Yorkshire Terrier's collar and should be around 15 feet (4.5 metres) in length.

The purpose of the training line is to prevent your Yorkshire Terrier from disobeying you so

that he never has the chance to get into bad habits. For example, when you call your Yorkie and he ignores you, you can immediately pick up the end of the training line and call him again. By picking up the line you will have attracted his attention and if you call in an excited, happy voice, your Yorkshire Terrier will come to you. The moment he reaches you, give him a tasty treat so he is instantly rewarded for making the 'right' decision.

When you have reinforced the correct behaviour a number of times, your dog will build up a strong recall and you will not need to use a training line.

WALKING ON A LOOSE LEAD

This is a simple exercise, and if you put in the training early on, you will soon have a dog who is happy to walk on a loose lead. In most cases, a Yorkshire Terrier will not try to pull, as this is not a breed that uses physical strength to get his own way. The most common problem is a Yorkie who continually stops to sniff, or one that keeps changing sides so you end up in a tangle.

In this exercise, as with all lessons that you teach your Yorkshire Terrier, you must adopt a calm, determined, no-nonsense attitude so he knows that you mean business. This is a dog who will run rings around you unless you earn his respect. Once this is established, your Yorkie will take you seriously and be happy to co-operate with you.

- In the early stages of lead training, allow your puppy to pick his route and follow him. He will get used to the feeling of being 'attached' to you and has no reason to put up any resistance.
- Next, find a toy or a tasty treat and show it to your puppy. Let him follow the treat/toy for a few paces and then reward him.
- Build up the amount of time your pup will walk with you, and, when he is walking nicely by your side, introduce the verbal command "Heel" or "Close". Give lots of praise when your pup is in the correct position.
- When your pup is walking alongside you, keep focusing

his attention on you by using his name and then rewarding him when he looks at you. If it is going well, introduce some changes of direction.
- Do not attempt to take your puppy out on the lead until you have mastered the basics at home. You need to be confident that your puppy accepts the lead and will focus his attention on you, when requested, before you face the challenge of a busy environment.
- If you are heading somewhere special, such as the park, your Yorkshire Terrier may become impatient and try to walk out in front of you. If this happens, stop, call your dog to you and do not set off again until he is in the correct position. It may take time, but your Yorkie will eventually realise that walking on a loose lead is pleasurable, compared with stopping and starting, which he will find as frustrating as you do.

STAYS

This may not be the most exciting exercise, but it is one of the most useful. There are many occasions when you want your Yorkshire Terrier to stay in

The aim is for your Yorkshire Terrier to walk on a lose lead, neither pulling ahead nor lagging behind.

position, even if it is only for a few seconds. The classic example is when you want your Yorkie to stay in the back of the car until you have clipped on his lead. This is such a high-energy breed that a dog who has not learnt to

Build up the Stay exercise in easy stages.

respond to "Stay" is a danger to himself and to others. Your Yorkie must learn to inhibit his exuberance and remain calm and still until he is released from the "Stay" position.

Some trainers use the verbal command "Stay" when the dog is to stay in position for an extended period of time and "Wait" if the dog is to stay in position for a few seconds until you give the next command. Other trainers use a universal "Stay" to cover all situations. It all comes down to personal preference, and as long as you are consistent, your dog will understand the command he is given.

• Put your puppy in a 'Sit' or a 'Down' and use a hand signal (flat palm, facing the dog) to show he is to stay in position. Step a pace away from the dog. Wait a second, step back and reward him. If you have a lively pup, you may find it easier to train this exercise on the lead.

• Repeat the exercise, gradually increasing the distance you can leave your dog. When you return to your dog's side, praise him quietly and release him with a command, such as "OK".

• Remember to keep your body language very still when you are training this exercise and avoid eye contact with your dog. Work on this exercise over a period of time and you will build up a really reliable 'Stay'.

SOCIALISATION

While your Yorkie is mastering basic obedience exercises, there is other, equally important work to do with him. A Yorkshire Terrier is not only becoming a part of your home and family, he is becoming a member of the community. He needs to be able to live in the outside world, coping calmly with every new situation that comes his way. This is particularly important if you see the world from your Yorkshire Terrier's perspective. He is a small dog that is learning to cope in a big world. He must not be treated like a baby or he may become nervous and apprehensive, picking up on your over-protective vibes. Equally, you need to remember that the Yorkie is a feisty little dog, and he must learn that he cannot take on the world… It is your job to introduce your Yorkshire Terrier to as many different experiences as possible and to encourage him to behave in an appropriate manner.

In order to socialise your Yorkie effectively, it is helpful to understand how his brain is developing and then you will get a perspective on how he sees the world.

CANINE SOCIALISATION
(Birth to 7 weeks)
This is the time when a dog learns how to be a dog. By interacting with his mother and his littermates, a young pup learns about leadership and submission. He learns to read body posture so that he

Puppies learn by playing with their littermates and interacting with their mother.

understands the intentions of his mother and his siblings. A puppy that is taken away from his litter too early may always have behavioural problems with other dogs, either being fearful or aggressive.

SOCIALISATION PERIOD
(7 to 12 weeks)

This is the time to get cracking and introduce your puppy to as many different experiences as possible. This includes meeting different people, other dogs and animals, seeing new sights and hearing a range of sounds, from the vacuum cleaner to the roar of traffic. A puppy learns very quickly and what he learns will stay with him for the rest of his life. This is the best time for a puppy to move to a new home, as he is adaptable and ready to form deep bonds.

FEAR-IMPRINT PERIOD
(8 to 11 weeks)

This occurs during the socialisation period and it can be the cause of problems if it is not handled carefully. If a pup is exposed to a frightening or painful experience, it will lead to lasting impressions. Obviously, you will attempt to avoid frightening situations, such as your pup being bullied by big dog, or a firework going off, but you cannot always protect your puppy from the unexpected. If your pup has a nasty experience, the best plan is to make light of it and distract him by offering him a treat or having a game. The pup will take the lead from you and will be reassured that there is nothing to worry about. If you mollycoddle him and sympathise with him, he is far more likely to retain the memory of his fear.

SENIORITY PERIOD
(12 to 16 weeks)

During this period, your puppy starts to cut the apron strings and becomes more independent. He will test out his status to find out who is the pack leader: him or you. Bad habits, such as play biting, which may have been seen as endearing a few weeks earlier, should be firmly discouraged. Remember to use positive, reward-based training, but make sure your puppy knows that you are the leader and must be respected.

SECOND FEAR-IMPRINT PERIOD (6 to 14 months)

This period is not as critical as the first fear-imprint period, but it should still be handled carefully. During this time your Yorkshire Terrier may appear apprehensive, or he may show fear of

A well-socialised Yorkie will be calm and confident in all situations.

something familiar. You may feel as if you have taken a backwards step, but if you adopt a calm, positive manner, your Yorkie will see that there is nothing to be frightened of. Do not make your dog confront the thing that frightens him. Simply distract his attention and give him something else to think about, such as obeying a simple command, such as "Sit" or "Down". This will give you the opportunity to praise and reward your dog and will help to boost his confidence.

YOUNG ADULTHOOD AND MATURITY (1 to 4 years)
The timing of this phase depends on the size of the dog: the bigger the dog, the later it is. This period coincides with a dog's increased size and strength, mental as well as physical. Some dogs, particularly those with a dominant nature, will test your leadership again and may become aggressive towards other dogs. Firmness and continued training are essential at this time, so that your Yorkshire Terrier accepts his status in the family pack.

IDEAS FOR SOCIALISATION
When you are socialising your Yorkshire Terrier, you want him to experience as many different situations as possible. Try out some of the following ideas, which will ensure he has an all-round education.

If you are taking on a rescued dog and have little knowledge of his background, it is important to work through a programme of socialisation. A young puppy soaks up new experiences like a sponge, but an older dog can still learn. If a rescued dog shows fear or apprehension, treat him in exactly the same way as you would treat a youngster who is going through the second fear-imprint period.

- Accustom your puppy to household noises, such as the vacuum cleaner, the television and the washing machine.
- Ask visitors to come to the door, wearing different types of clothing – for example, wearing a hat, a long raincoat, or carrying a stick or an umbrella.
- If you do not have children at home, make sure your Yorkshire Terrier has a chance to meet and play with them. Go to a local park and watch children in the play area. You will not be able to take your Yorkshire Terrier inside the play area, but he will see children playing and will get used to their shouts of excitement.
- Attend puppy classes. These are designed for puppies between the ages of 12 to 20 weeks and give puppies a chance to play and interact together in a controlled, supervised environment. Your vet will have details of a local class.
- Take a walk around some quiet streets, such as a residential area, so your Yorkshire Terrier can get used to the sound of traffic. As he becomes more confident, progress to busier areas. Remember, your lead is like a live wire and your feelings will travel directly to

your Yorkie. Assume a calm, confident manner and your puppy will take the lead from you and have no reason to be fearful.

- Go to a railway station. You don't have to get on a train if you don't need to, but your Yorkshire Terrier will have the chance to experience trains, people wheeling luggage, loudspeaker announcements and going up and down stairs and over railway bridges.
- If you live in the town, plan a trip to the country. You can enjoy a day out and provide an opportunity for your Yorkshire Terrier to see livestock, such as sheep, cattle and horses.
- One of the best places for socialising a dog is at a country

fair. There will be crowds of people, livestock in pens, tractors, bouncy castles, fairground rides and food stalls.
- When your dog is over 20 weeks of age, locate a training class for adult dogs. You may find that your nearest training club has both puppy and adult classes.

THE ADOLESCENT YORKSHIRE TERRIER

It happens to every dog – and every owner. One minute you have an obedient, well-behaved youngster and the next you have a boisterous adolescent who appears to have forgotten everything he ever learnt.

The age at which Yorkshire Terriers become adolescent, and

when they reach maturity, varies tremendously from individual to individual. It does seem to be influenced by bloodlines, so the best person to advise you is your Yorkie's breeder. A Yorkshire Terrier male may show adolescent behaviour at any time from six months, but he may show no signs until he is 12 months of age. In terms of behavioural changes, a male often becomes more boisterous in play, and he will start to 'mark' his territory. He may also become more assertive as he tests the boundaries.

Female Yorkshire Terriers may have a first season as early as six months of age or it may be closer to 12 months of age. Again, the age this happens often depends

TRAINING CLUBS

There are lots of training clubs to choose from. Your vet will probably have details of clubs in your area, or you can ask friends who have dogs if they attend a club. Alternatively, use the internet to find out more information. But how do you know if the club is any good?

Before you take your dog, ask if you can go to a class as an observer and find out the following:
- What experience does the instructor(s) have?
- Do they have experience with Yorkshire Terriers?
- Is the class well organised and are the dogs

reasonably quiet? (A noisy class indicates an unruly atmosphere, which will not be conducive to learning.)
- Are there are a number of classes to suit dogs of different ages and abilities?
- Are positive, reward-based training methods used?
- Does the club train for the Good Citizen Scheme (see page 104)?

If you are not happy with the training club, find another one. An inexperienced instructor who cannot handle a number of dogs in a confined environment can do more harm than good.

As your Yorkie starts to mature, he may question your role as leader.

on bloodlines as well as individual maturity. An adolescent female may become possessive over toys, and if you have a male in the house, she may try to 'guard' the toys so he cannot get them. In general, a female will mature earlier than a male. In most cases, a female starts to mature noticeably after her first season. A male may be 18 months or even two years old before he reaches full maturity.

Adolescence can be a trying time, but it is important to retain a sense of perspective. Look at the situations from the dog's perspective and respond to uncharacteristic behaviour with firmness and consistency. Just like a teenager, an adolescent Yorkshire feels the need to flex his muscles and challenge the status quo. But if you show that you are a strong leader (see page 82) and are quick to reward good behaviour, your Yorkie will be happy to accept you as his protector and provider.

WHEN THINGS GO WRONG

Positive, reward-based training has proved to be the most effective method of teaching dogs, but what happens when your Yorkshire Terrier does something wrong and you need to show him that his behaviour is unacceptable? The old-fashioned school of dog training used to rely on the powers of punishment and negative reinforcement. A dog who raided the bin, for example, was smacked. Now we have learnt that it is not only unpleasant and cruel to hit a dog, it is also ineffective. If you hit a dog for stealing, he is more than likely to see you as the bad consequence of stealing, so he may raid the bin again, but probably not when you are around. If he raided the bin some time before you discovered it, he will be even more confused by your punishment, as he will not relate your response to his 'crime'.

A more commonplace example is when a dog fails to respond to a recall in the park. When the dog eventually comes back, the owner puts the dog on the lead and goes straight home to punish the dog for his poor response. Unfortunately, the dog will have a different interpretation. He does not think: "I won't ignore a recall command because the bad consequence is the end of my play in the park." He thinks: "Coming to my owner resulted in the end of playtime – therefore, coming to my owner has a bad consequence, so I won't do that again."

There are a number of strategies to tackle undesirable behaviour – and they have nothing to do with harsh handling.

There may be times when your Yorkshire Terrier develops selective hearing when he find something more interesting to do.

Ignoring bad behaviour: The Yorkshire Terrier is a people dog, and is very good at tuning into his owner's feelings. He enjoys being praised, and if you have earned his respect, he will not feel the need to thwart your authority. However, if he picks up on weakness or hesitancy, he may decide to turn a situation to his advantage. For example, a Yorkshire Terrier may try to get your attention – and if he doesn't get it, he may demand it by barking at you. He believes he can change a situation simply by making a noise – and this strategy will usually work, as you will give him your attention to tell him to be quiet. He will not see that he is being reprimanded. As far as he is concerned, he is getting the attention he wants, so why inhibit his behaviour?

In this situation, the best and most effective response is to ignore your Yorkshire Terrier. Do not talk to him, do not go near him, and avoid all eye contact. When your Yorkie is calm and quiet, you can give him some attention, but keep it quiet and low key. Repeat this on every occasion when your Yorkshire Terrier barks to demand attention, and he will soon learn that barking is non-productive. He is not rewarded with your attention – and it will not take long for him to realise that being quiet is the most effective strategy. In this scenario, you have not only taught your Yorkshire Terrier not to demand attention, you have also earned his respect because you have taken control of the situation.

Stopping bad behaviour: There are occasions when you want to call an instant halt to whatever it is your Yorkshire Terrier is doing. He may have just jumped on the sofa, or you may have caught him red-handed in the rubbish bin. He has already committed the 'crime', so your aim is to stop him and to redirect his attention. You can do this by using a deep, firm tone of voice to say "No", which will startle him, and then call him to you in a bright, happy voice. If necessary, you can attract him with a toy or a treat. The moment your Yorkie stops the undesirable behaviour and comes towards you, you can reward his good behaviour. You can back this up by running through a couple of simple exercises, such as a 'Sit' or a 'Down' and rewarding with treats. In this way, your Yorkshire Terrier focuses his attention on you and sees you as the greatest source of reward and pleasure.

In a more extreme situation, when you want to interrupt undesirable behaviour and you know that a simple "No" will not do the trick, you can try something a little more dramatic. If you get a can and fill it with pebbles, it will make a really loud noise when you shake it or throw it. The same effect can be achieved with purpose-made training discs. The dog will be startled and stop what he is doing. Even better, the dog will not associate the unpleasant noise with you. This gives you the perfect opportunity to be the nice guy, calling the dog to you and giving him lots of praise.

PROBLEM BEHAVIOUR

If you have trained your Yorkshire Terrier from puppyhood, survived his adolescence and established yourself as a fair and consistent leader, you will end up with a

A Yorkshire Terrier thrives on attention – but he should not be allowed to demand it.

brilliant companion dog. The Yorkshire Terrier is a well-balanced dog, who rarely has hang-ups if he has been correctly reared and socialised. The most common reason for problem behaviour among Yorkshire Terriers is over-indulgent, inconsistent owners. An owner who spoils and pampers a Yorkie will end up with a dog who seeks to take advantage – and if he doesn't get his own way, he will register his disapproval with a discontented growl. This has nothing to do with the typical Yorkshire Terrier temperament, which is second to none; it is the fault of the owner who has failed

to establish the correct hierarchy in the family pack.

If you have taken on a rescued Yorkie, it may be that you are having to cope with established behavioural problems that are the result of poor management in a former home. If this is the case, or if you are worried about your Yorkshire Terrier and feel out of your depth, do not delay in seeking professional help. This is readily available, usually through a referral from your vet, or you can find out additional information on the internet (see Appendices for web addresses). An animal behaviourist will have experience in tackling problem behaviour and will be able to help both you and your dog.

DOMINANCE/RESOURCE GUARDING

If you have trained and socialised your Yorkshire Terrier correctly, he will know his place in the family pack and will have no desire to challenge your authority. If you have taken on a rescued dog who has not been trained and socialised, or if you have been inconsistent in handling your Yorkshire Terrier, you may find you have problems with a dominant dog.

It is a mistake to believe that it is only the big, macho breeds, such as Rottweilers or German Shepherd Dogs, that show dominant behaviour. Certainly, a big dog has the muscle to back up his feelings, but, in fact, dominance is expressed in many different ways, which may include the following:

An assertive Yorkie may try to 'guard' his prized possessions.

You need to teach your Yorkie that you 'own' his toys and he must give them up on request.

- Showing lack of respect for your personal space. For example, your Yorkie will always be prancing at your heels, or running ahead so he can go through doors ahead of you.
- Ignoring basic obedience commands.
- Showing no respect to younger members of the family, jumping up at them, mouthing them or trying to steal their toys.
- A male dogs may start marking (cocking his leg) in the house.
- Aggression towards people or other dogs (see page 104).

However, the most common behaviour displayed by a Yorkshire Terrier who has ideas above his station is resource guarding. This may take a number of different forms:

- Getting up on to the sofa or your favourite armchair and growling when you tell him to get back on the floor.
- Becoming possessive over a toy, or guarding his food bowl by growling when you get too close.
- Growling when anyone approaches his bed or when anyone gets too close to where he is lying.

In each of these scenarios, the Yorkshire Terrier has something he values and he aims to keep it. He does not have sufficient respect for you, his human leader, to give up what he wants and he is 'warning' you to keep away.

If you see signs of your Yorkie behaving in this way, you must work at lowering his status so that he realises that you are the leader and he must accept your authority. Although you need to be firm, you also need to use positive training methods so that your Yorkshire Terrier is rewarded for the behaviour you want. In this way, his 'correct' behaviour will be strengthened and repeated.

The golden rule is not to become confrontational. The dog will see this as a challenge and may become even more determined not to co-operate. There are a number of steps you can take to lower your Yorkshire Terrier's status, which are far more likely to have a successful outcome. They include:

- Go back to basics and hold daily training sessions. Make sure you have some really tasty treats, or find a toy your Yorkie really values and only bring it out at training sessions. Run through all the training exercises you have taught your Yorkshire Terrier, making it a

fun session, which will give him mental stimulation and give you the opportunity to make a big fuss of him and reward him when he does well. This will help to reinforce the message that you are the leader and that it is rewarding to do as you ask.

- Teach your Yorkshire Terrier something new; this can be as simple as learning a trick, such as shaking paws. A Yorkie loves

to show off, and he will benefit from interacting with you.

- Be 100 per cent consistent with all house rules – your Yorkshire Terrier must *never* sit on the sofa and you must *never* allow him to guard his favourite toy. Whatever breed of dog you train, consistency is important, but most owners agree that it is crucial with a Yorkshire Terrier. The quick-thinking Yorkie will sum up a situation in a split

SEPARATION ANXIETY

A Yorkshire Terrier should be brought up to accept short periods of separation from his owner so that he does not become anxious. A new puppy should be left for short periods on his own, ideally in a crate where he cannot get up to any mischief. It is a good idea to leave him with a boredom-busting toy so he will be happily occupied in your absence. When you return, do not rush to the crate and make a huge fuss. Wait a few minutes, and then calmly go to the crate and release your dog, telling him how good he has been. If this scenario is repeated a number of times, your Yorkie will soon learn that being left on his own is no big deal.

Problems with separation anxiety are most likely to arise if you take on a rescued dog who has major insecurities. You may also find your Yorkshire Terrier hates being left if you have failed to accustom him to short periods of isolation when he was growing up. Separation anxiety is expressed in a number of ways and all are equally distressing for both dog and owner. An

anxious dog who is left alone may bark and whine continuously, urinate and defecate, and may be extremely destructive. The Yorkshire Terrier may even sulk when his owners return and refuse food at his next mealtime.

There are a number of steps you can take when attempting to solve this problem.

- Put up a baby-gate between adjoining rooms and leave your dog in one room while you are in the other room. Your dog will be able to see you and hear you, but he is learning to cope without being right next to you. Build up the amount of time you can leave your dog in easy stages.
- Buy some boredom-busting toys and fill them with some tasty treats. Whenever you leave your dog, give him a food-filled toy so that he is busy while you are away.
- If you have not used a crate before, it is not too late to start. Make sure the crate is cosy and train your Yorkshire Terrier to get used to going in his crate while you are in the same room.

second, and if he senses weakness or inconsistency, he will be swift to take advantage.

- If your Yorkshire Terrier is becoming possessive over toys, remove all his toys and keep them out of reach. It is then up to you to decide when to produce a toy and to initiate a game. Equally, it is you who will decide when the game is over and when to remove the toy. This teaches your Yorkshire Terrier that you 'own' his toys. He has fun playing and interacting with you, but the game is over – and the toy is given up – when you say so.

- If your Yorkie has been guarding his food bowl, put the bowl down empty and drop in a little food at a time. Periodically stop dropping in the food and tell your Yorkshire Terrier to "Sit" and "Wait". Give it a few seconds and then reward him by dropping in more food. This shows your Yorkie that you are the provider of the food and he can only eat when you allow him to.

- Make sure the family eats before you feed your Yorkie. Some trainers advocate eating in front of the dog (maybe just a few bites from a biscuit) before starting a training session, so the dog appreciates your elevated status.

Gradually build up the amount of time he spends in the crate and then start leaving the room for short periods. When you return, do not make a fuss of your dog. Leave him for five or ten minutes before releasing him, so that he gets used to your comings and goings.

- Pretend to go out, putting on your coat and jangling keys, but do not leave the house. An anxious dog often becomes hyped up by the ritual of leaving and this will help to desensitize him.

- When you go out, leave a radio or a TV on. Some dogs are comforted by hearing voices and background noise when they are left alone.

- Try to make your absences as short as possible when you are first training your dog to accept being on his own.

If you take these steps, your dog should become less anxious and, over a period of time, you should be able to solve the problem. However, if you are failing to make progress, do not delay in calling in expert help.

If you use a stair gate, your Yorkie will still be able to see you, but is learning to be more independent.

AGGRESSION

Aggression is a complex issue, as there are different causes and the behaviour may be triggered by numerous factors. It may be directed towards people, but far more commonly it is directed towards other dogs. Aggression in dogs may be the result of:

- Dominance (see page 100).
- Defensive behaviour: This may be induced by fear, pain or punishment.
- Territory: A dog may become aggressive if strange dogs or people enter his territory (which is generally seen as the house and garden).
- Intra-sexual issues: This is aggression between sexes – male-to-male or female-to-female.
- Parental instinct: A mother dog may become aggressive if she is protecting her puppies.

The Yorkshire Terrier is an out-going, friendly dog, and rarely has problems relating to other dogs. As already noted, problems may arise if a larger dog gets flustered and confused by the attentions of a fearless Yorkie who is full of confidence and self-assurance. However, if you allow your puppy to mix with other dogs of sound temperament from an early age, it will give him the chance to learn good canine manners that other dogs will understand.

However, you may have taken on an older, rescued dog that has been poorly socialised and there is something in his history that has made him aggressive. Or you may have a dog who has become dominant in his own home and family and so he is assertive in his dealings with other dogs. This sometimes happens if you are keeping a number of dogs, and one decides he wants to take on the role of top dog.

If dominance is the underlying cause, you can try the measures outlined in this chapter. Equally, if your dog has been poorly socialised, you can try to make up for lost time and work with other dogs of sound temperament in controlled situations. But if you are concerned about your dog's behaviour, you would be well advised to call in professional help. If the aggression is directed towards people, you should seek immediate advice. This behaviour can escalate very quickly and could lead to disastrous consequences.

- Do not let your Yorkshire Terrier run through doors ahead of you or leap from the back of the car before you release him. You may need to put your dog on the lead and teach him to "Wait" at doorways, or in the back of the car, and then reward him when you have given the release command.

If your Yorkshire Terrier is progressing well with his retraining programme, think about giving him additional stimulation by joining a training club, or maybe having a go at a dog sport, such as agility. This will give your Yorkshire Terrier a positive outlet for his energies. However, if your Yorkie is still seeking to be dominant, or you have any other concerns, do not delay in seeking the help of an animal behaviourist.

NEW CHALLENGES

If you enjoy training your Yorkshire Terrier you may want to try one of the many dog sports that are now on offer. Obviously, a Toy dog will not be able to participate in the sports designed for bigger dogs, but you will be surprised by what you can achieve with a well-trained Yorkie.

GOOD CITIZEN SCHEME

This is a scheme run by the

If your Yorkshire Terrier is responding well to training, why not try a new challenge?

Kennel Club in the UK and the American Kennel Club in the USA. The schemes promote responsible ownership and help you to train a well-behaved dog who will fit in with the community. The schemes are excellent for all pet owners and they are also a good starting point if you plan to compete with your Yorkshire Terrier when he is older. The KC and the AKC schemes vary in format. In the UK there are three levels: bronze, silver and gold, with each test becoming progressively more demanding. In the AKC scheme there is a single test.

Some of the exercises include:
- Walking on a loose lead among people and other dogs.
- Recall amid distractions.
- A controlled greeting where dogs stay under control while their owners meet.
- The dog allows all-over grooming and handling by his owner, and also accepts being handled by the examiner.
- Stays, with the owner in sight and then out of sight.
- Food manners, allowing the owner to eat without begging and taking a treat on command.

- Sendaway – sending the dog to his bed.

The tests are designed to show the control you have over your dog and his ability to respond correctly and remain calm in all situations. The Good Citizen Scheme is taught at most training clubs. For more information, log on to the Kennel Club or AKC website (see Appendices).

SHOWING

In your eyes, your Yorkshire Terrier is the most beautiful dog in the world – but would a judge agree? Showing is a highly competitive sport and, at the top level, presentation is all important. However, many owners get bitten by the showing bug, and their calendar is governed by the dates of the top showing fixtures.

To be successful in the show ring, a Yorkshire Terrier must conform as closely as possible to the Breed Standard, which is a written blueprint describing the 'perfect' Yorkshire Terrier (see Chapter Seven). To get started you need to buy a puppy that has show potential and then train him to perform in the ring. A Yorkshire Terrier will be expected to stand in show pose, gait for the judge in order to show off his natural movement, and to be examined by the judge. This involves a detailed hands-on examination, so your Yorkie must be bombproof when handled by strangers.

Many training clubs hold ringcraft classes, which are run by experienced showgoers. At these classes, you will learn how to handle your Yorkshire Terrier in the ring, and you will also find out about rules, procedures and show ring etiquette.

The best plan is to start off at some small, informal shows,

Showing at the top level is highly competitive.

A larger, more robust Yorkie can compete in Agility.

where you can practise and learn the tricks of the trade, before graduating to bigger shows. It's a long haul starting in the very first puppy class, but the dream is to make your Yorkshire Terrier a Champion.

AGILITY

This fun sport has grown enormously in popularity over the past few years, and the bigger type of Yorkshire Terrier, who is slightly more substantial than a show dog, is perfectly capable of competing in the classes for small dogs.

In agility competitions, each dog must complete a set course over a series of obstacles. These can include the following:
• Jumps (upright hurdles and long jump, varying in height – small, medium and large, depending on the size of the dog)
• Weaves
• A-frame
• Dog walk
• Seesaw
• Tunnels (collapsible and rigid)
• Tyre

Dogs may compete in jumping classes, with jumps, tunnels and weaves, or in agility classes, which have the full set of equipment. Faults are awarded for poles down on the jumps, missed contact points on the A-frame, dog walk and seesaw, and refusals. If a dog takes the wrong course, he is eliminated. The winner is the dog that completes the course in the fastest time with no faults. As you progress up the levels, courses become progressively harder with more twists, turns and changes of direction.

If you want to get involved in agility, you will need to find a club that specialises in the sport (see Appendices). You will not be allowed to start training until your Yorkshire Terrier is 12 months old and you cannot compete until he is 18 months old. This rule is for the protection of the dog, who may suffer injury if he puts strain on bones and joints while he is still growing.

COMPETITIVE OBEDIENCE

In the UK, this sport is dominated by Border Collies, German Shepherd Dogs and some of the Gundog breeds. However, in other countries –

particularly in the USA – owners of Toy dogs are keen to have a go, and many achieve a fair degree of success. The classes start off at beginner level and become increasingly complex as dog and handler become more advanced. The exercises that must be mastered include the following:

- **Heelwork:** Dog and handler must complete a set pattern on and off the lead, which includes left turns, right turns, about turns and changes of pace.
- **Recall:** This may be when the handler is stationary or on the move.
- **Retrieve:** This may be a dumbbell or any article chosen by the judge.
- **Sendaway:** The dog is sent to a designated spot and must go into an instant 'Down' until he is recalled by the handler.
- **Stays:** The dog must stay in the 'Sit' and in the 'Down' for a

set amount of time. In advanced classes, the handler is out of sight.
- **Scent:** The dog must retrieve a single cloth from a pre-arranged pattern of cloths that has his owner's scent or, in advanced classes, the judge's scent. There may also be decoy cloths.
- **Distance control.** The dog must execute a series of moves ('Sit', 'Stand', 'Down') without moving from his position and with the handler at a distance.

Even though competitive obedience requires accuracy and precision, make sure you make it fun for your Yorkshire Terrier, with lots of praise and rewards so that you motivate him to do his best. Many training clubs run advanced classes for those who want to compete in obedience, or you can hire the services of a professional trainer for one-on-one sessions.

DANCING WITH DOGS

This sport is relatively new, but it is becoming increasingly popular. It is very entertaining to watch, but it is certainly not as simple as it looks. To perform a choreographed routine to music with your Yorkshire Terrier demands a huge amount of training.

Dancing with dogs is divided into two categories: heelwork to music and canine freestyle. In heelwork to music, the dog must work closely with his handler and show a variety of close 'heelwork' positions. In canine freestyle, the routine can be more flamboyant, with the dog working at a distance from the handler and performing spectacular tricks. Routines are judged on style and presentation, content and accuracy.

You may decide to have a go at Rally O, which is a relatively new sport that began in the USA. In this, dogs compete in a variety of exercises, going from stage to stage, until the finish when points are calculated. The exercises are more varied than in Competitive Obedience, and accuracy is not of such paramount importance.

SUMMING UP

The Yorkshire Terrier is a breed like no other – he is intelligent, fun-loving, feisty and loyal. Make sure you keep your half of the bargain: spend time socialising and training your Yorkshire Terrier so you establish a mutual sense of trust and respect, and you will have a dog that you can take anywhere and who will always be a credit to you.

The work you put into training when your Yorkie is growing up will pay off handsomely when he matures into an outstanding companion dog.

THE PERFECT YORKSHIRE TERRIER

Chapter 7

The Breed Standard is a picture in words of what the 'perfect' Yorkshire Terrier should look like. It is the template used by judges, breeders and exhibitors to perpetuate the breed so that it remains a true 'Yorkshire Terrier' in terms of conformation, coat, colour movement and temperament.

The Kennel Club (KC) in the UK has its own Breed Standard handed down from those who founded and developed the breed, with a number of minor changes introduced at various stages in its history. The KC Breed Standard is concise and leaves a lot scope for interpretation by judges and breeders alike. In recent years, there have been two major changes. In April 2007 tail docking was banned in the UK, and now all dogs born after this date must be shown with a full tail. A clause was also introduced stating that, with written permission, dogs that had been spayed or castrated could be shown. More recently, in January 2009, the UK Kennel Club revised its Breed Standards and introduced the following clause:

"A Breed Standard is the guideline which describes the ideal characteristics, temperament and appearance of a breed and ensures that the breed is fit for function. Absolute soundness is essential. Breeders and judges should at all times be careful to avoid obvious conditions or exaggerations which would be detrimental in any way to the health, welfare or soundness of this breed.

"From time to time, certain conditions or exaggerations may be considered to have the potential to affect dogs in some breeds adversely, and judges and breeders are requested to refer to the Kennel Club website for details of any such current issues. If a feature or quality is desirable it should only be present in the right measure."

In the USA, the Yorkshire Terrier is a very popular breed, and is shown in the Toy Group, the same as in the UK. The American Breed Standard, drawn up by the American Kennel Club (AKC) is slightly different to the United Kingdom and more detailed, but remains very much the same in substance. It is only in the show ring that there is an apparent difference, and that is in preparation and the tying of the top-knot. You will also see ribbons of other colours rather than the tradtional red, which is used in the UK. In the United States, Yorkshire Terriers show on the red box, as is the custom in the United Kingdom. Professional handlers are often used, whereas

Top-winning
UK dog Ch.
Ozmilion Love
in Your Eyes.

Am. Ch. Mistangay
Boom Boom: Highly
successful in the
American show ring.

Int. Ch. Vive La France du Gue L'Adour: A top winner under FCI rules.

in the UK most breeders prefer to show their own stock.

The Federation Cynologique Internationale (FCI), which covers most other countries, adopts the Breed Standard according to the country of origin. The Yorkshire Terrier is a British breed, and therefore the FCI judges to this Standard.

THE SHOW WORLD

To start showing is quite an adventure. Most people start at the bottom, with small open or limit shows or breed shows, which means that one breed is allowed at the show. To enter shows you need a schedule.

This is your entry, which has to be filled in and sent to the secretary of the particular club holding the show. When you sign the entry form, you are agreeing to abide by the rules of the governing Kennel Club. Maybe when you have had some success at this level you will feel confident enough to enter a Championship show. Once again, at this level, it will be all-breed or single-breed shows. These shows continue all the year through and all across the country.

When you show your dog, the judge has helpers in the show ring with him and they are

called 'stewards'. They help to organise the classes, making sure dogs and exhibitors appear in the right class at the right time. They give out numbers and check that no one is in the show ring when they should not be. When the judge has finished the class and placed his winners, the steward hands out cards or rosettes and calls in the next class.

All this might make the novice wary of starting down the road of showing, but most areas have a training club run by show people, which is affiliated to the Kennel Club. This is truly the first step on

what will, hopefully, lead to a glittering career.

While a Toy dog, and at various times a greatly pampered one, the Yorkshire Terrier is a spirited dog that definitely shows its terrier strain. The show dog's length of coat makes constant care necessary to protect it from damage, but the breed is happy to engage in all the roistering activities of the larger terrier breeds. It is important to bear this in mind, so your Yorkshire Terrier enjoys life to the full, as well as being the most glamorous of all show dogs.

A Yorkshire Terrier in full coat can still enjoy life to the full. This is Ch. Jankeri Blue Iris.

HEALTH ISSUES

The breed does have a few inherited problems, and responsible breeders work tirelessly to eliminate these from their breeding programmes. The aim is to produce the 'perfect' Yorkshire Terrier and this means breeding dogs that are sound in mind and body, as well as conforming to the stipulations of the Breed Standard.

The inherited conditions that breeders should be aware of include the following:

- **Slipping patella:** This is a condition where a dog has loose kneecaps – as the dog walks, the back leg will hop. This can be serious and require surgery or it may be so minor that the dog can cope very well.
- **Undershot or overshot mouths:** In an undershot mouth, the top jaw is shorter than the bottom; with an overshot mouth, the top jaw is much longer than the bottom. Surprisingly, in both cases the dog can usually eat as normal.
- **Entropion:** This is when the eyelashes grow inside the eye-rim and causes discomfort for the dog.
- **Heart disease:** This can be quite common in the older dog but once again different ratios take different medication.
- **Teeth:** Yorkies can suffer from ginigivitis. Keeping teeth clean will prevent this.
- **Progressive Retinal Atrophy:** This eye defect may affect the Yorkshire Terrier and there are various schemes in operation to test for the disorder (see page 142).

For more information, see Chapter Eight: Happy and Healthy.

THE JUDGE'S EXAMINATION

In the show ring the judge conducts a 'hands-on' examination of each dog to see how closely he conforms to the Breed Standard.

The judge will take in the overall picture as the dog is posed on the table.

Every judge has their own method, but the aim is to work systematically, assessing how each dog is put together.

The judge will brush through the coat to evaluate colour and texture.

The dog will be 'moved' so that the judge can look at his gaiit.

Time to decide: The judge has a final look at the exhibits before deciding which dog, in her opinion, best fits the description of the 'perfect' Yorkshire Terrier, given in the Breed Standard.

ANALYSIS & INTERPRETATION OF THE BREED STANDARD

GENERAL APPEARANCE, CHARACTERSTICS AND TEMPERAMENT

KC

GENERAL APPEARANCE
Long-coated, coat hanging quite straight and evenly down each side, a parting extending from the nose to the end of the tail. Very compact and neat, carriage very upright conveying an important air. General outline conveying impression of vigorous and well proportioned body.

CHARACTERSITICS
Alert, intelligent toy terrier.

TEMPERAMENT
Spirited with even disposition.

AKC

GENERAL APPEARANCE
That of a long-haired toy terrier whose blue and tan coat is parted on the face and from the base of the skull to the end of the tail and hangs evenly and quite straight down each side of the body. The body is neat, compact and well proportioned. The dog's high head carriage and confident manner should give the appearance of vigour and self-importance.

The AKC places much more importance on head carriage than the KC, but both Standards are clearly looking for an intelligent expression.

The head proportions are small and flat – not too round in the skull, and not too long in the muzzle.

HEAD AND SKULL

KC
Rather small and flat, not too prominent or round in skull, not too long in muzzle, with black nose.

EYES
Medium, dark, sparkling with

intelligent expression and placed to look directly forward. Not prominent. Edge of eyelids dark.

EARS
Small v-shaped, carried erect, not too far apart, and covered with short hair, colour very deep rich tan.

MOUTH
Perfect regular and complete scissor bite; i.e. upper teeth closely overlapping lower teeth and set square to the jaw. Teeth well placed with even jaws.

AKC
Small and rather flat on top, the *skull* not too prominent or round, the *muzzle* not too long, with the *bite* neither undershot nor overshot and teeth sound. Either scissors bite or level bite is acceptable.
The *nose* is black.
Eyes are medium in size and not too prominent; dark in color and sparkling with a sharp, intelligent expression. Eye rims are dark. Ears are small, V-shaped, carried erect and set not too far apart.

"Rather small and flat" in this breed is very important. We do not want a head that is too bold and cumbersome. A small, flat head will also make the dog look more elegant. The skull should not be too round or prominent, as it will give the appearance of a Chihuahua. The muzzle should be about a third of the skull depth, so one-third muzzle to

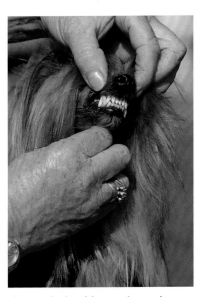

The teeth should meet in a scissor bite, with the teeth on the upper jaw closely over-lapping the teeth on the lower jaw.

two-thirds skull. The nose should be black, not brown or pink shading.

Eyes should be of medium size and, when showing, a dog should look as though he is interested in what is going on. Many can give the blank "I'm not interested look". The eyes should be sparkling – this always indicates a healthy dog – and the rims around the eyes can accentuate the expression.

Ears should be small and V-shaped, covered in rich, tan coat. They need to 'fit in' with the rest of the dog's head. If they are too large, they will give the appearance of being top heavy and are more likely to flop, or to be very wide at the base. The ears

should sit about 10 to 2 at the widest, or 5 to 1 to give an alert appearance.

A perfect and regular bite is what is being looked for. This means that the top jaw is neither too long for the bottom teeth, nor too short for the bottom teeth. The top teeth should just meet and fit very close to the bottom teeth. The teeth should be even and well set in the jaws. There should be six teeth on the top and bottom jaws between incisors – these are the long teeth halfway along the dog's jaw-line.

NECK AND BODY

KC
NECK
Good reach of neck.

BODY
Compact with moderate spring of rib, good loin. Level back.

AKC
BODY
Well proportioned and very compact. The back is rather short, the back line level, with height at shoulder the same as at the rump.

The neck should have a good reach. This means that if you put your hand on the neck, you can get three or four fingers between the back of the ears and down to the body or shoulder placement. Having a good reach will give the dog an air of elegance.

Moderate spring of rib is called for. This is, again, a necessity, as a good body holds the engine to the dog. Not enough spring of rib will make the dog flat or slab-sided; too much and the dog will look like a little barrel on legs. A good indication on a mature dog is to put your thumbs and first fingers together and make a soft 'V' or 'U'. The loin is the part between the finish of the rib and the start of the hip. Placing fingers between this gap will give you an indication of whether a dog is long or short in loin. If it is strong and muscled, it shows that the dog has plenty of exercise. If not, lack of exercise is often the reason. Also, at this point, you can access how level the back is.

FOREQUARTERS, HINDQUARTERS, FEET

KC
FOREQUARTERS
Well laid shoulders, legs straight, well covered with hair of rich golden tan a few shades lighter at ends than at the rots, not extending higher on forelegs than elbow.

HINDQUARTERS
Legs quite straight when viewed from behind, moderate turn of stifle. Well covered with rich golden tan a few shades lighter at ends than at roots, not extending higher on hind legs than stifles.

FEET
Round, nails black.

AKC
LEGS AND FEET
Forelegs should be straight, elbows neither in nor out. Hind legs straight when viewed from behind, but stifles are moderately bent when viewed from the sides. Feet are round with black toenails. Dewclaws, if any, are generally removed from the hind legs. Dewclaws on the forelegs may be removed.

The body is very compact, and the topline is level.

The rich, tan coat on the legs should be a few shades lighter at the ends than at the roots.

The front of the dog, or forequarters, are the start of the shape of his body. The lay of shoulder will determine how a dog moves at the front. If he is too upright in shoulder, it will change all the bone structure at the front. Elbows will be out at the side of the dog and, when walking, will appear to plait (cross one leg over the other). The legs when viewed from the front should be straight when standing and walking.

Now on to the hindquarters. Once again, putting your hands on the dog will show you how much muscle the dog has. Legs, when viewed from the back, should be straight. If they look 'cow-hocked,' turning in at the knee, or pigeon-toed, this is a major fault. When viewed from the side there should be a good turn of stifle; this gives the dog the strength to drive along when moving. If the stifle is too straight, the dog appears to tip-toe and does not extend the leg. Often, it appears that the dog is bouncing rather than flowing. Too much stifle and the dog appears 'bum high' when standing, and often over-extends or crabs when walking. The legs should fit under the rear of the dog and it should not stand like a German Shepherd Dog.

The feet should be rounded and cat-like with black nails. If the feet are hare-like or oval, they can appear flat-footed. But with

GAIT & MOVEMENT

The judge will look at a dog from different angles to see if he has the correct movement.

small, round feet, the dog appears to be dancing across the floor.

KC
TAIL
Undocked – plenty of hair, darker blue in colour than rest of body, especially at the end of tail. Carried a little higher than level of back. As straight as possible. Length to give a well-balanced appearance.

AKC
Docked to medium length and carried slightly higher than the level of the back.

Tail docking is still allowed in the United States. It has been banned in the United Kingdom since April 2007. Therefore, the Breed Standard description for the tail is still relatively new to British exhibitors.

The tail is an extension of the body, not carried too low or too high like a jug handle. It is darker blue than the rest of the body. It does accentuate the topline; it certainly determines that if a dog has a low tail set he will appear more like a Dachshund. If it is a gay tail, with the tail carried over the back, you get the appearance of a Maltese tail.

It is interesting to note that part of Breed Standard could change in a few years' time when it becomes clear what breeders are trying to achieve.

GAIT/MOVEMENT

KC
Free with drive, straight action front and behind, retaining level topline.

AKC
No directive given.

The American Breed Standard does not describe movement, so we must turn to the British version for an explanation. As has been stated previously, the shape will determine how the dog moves. A free and easy movement, seen from the side, will probably show just a flick of legs and feet in a full-coated animal. On a cut-coated dog you

At 18 months of age, this Yorkshire Terrier has yet to develop his full coat.

The full coat reaches right down to ground level.

will get an extension from the shoulder straight through to the foot at the front, and an extension from the thigh, stifle and foot at the back. The dog will appear to flow along the ground. You will also notice how level the topline is at this point.

COAT AND COLOUR

KC
COAT
Hair on body moderately long, perfectly straight (not wavy), glossy, fine silky texture, not woolly. Fall on head long, rich golden tan deeper in colour at sides of head, about ear roots and on muzzle where it should be very long. Tan on head not to extend on to neck, nor must any sooty or dark hair intermingle with any tan.

COLOUR
Dark steel blue (not silver blue) extending from occiput to root of tail, never mingled with fawn, bronze or dark hairs. Hair on chest rich bright tan. All hair darker at roots than in middle, shading to still lighter at tips.

AKC
COAT
Quality, texture and quantity of coat are of prime importance. Hair glossy, fine and silky in texture. Coat on the body is moderately long and perfectly straight (not wavy). It may be trimmed to floor length to give ease of movement and neater appearance, if desired. The fall on the head is long, tied with

122

one bow in centre of head or parted in the middle and tied with two bows. Hair on muzzle is very long. Hair should be trimmed short on tips of ears and may be trimmed on feet to give them a neat appearance.

COLORS
Puppies are born black and tan and are normally darker in body color, showing an intermingling of black hair in the tan until they are matured. Color of hair on body and richness of tan on head and legs are of prime importance in adult dogs, to which the following colour requirements apply:
Blue: is a dark steel blue, not silver-blue and not mingled with fawn, bronzy or black hairs.
Tan: All tan hair is darker at the roots than in the middle, shading to still lighter tan at the tips. There should be no sooty or black hair intermingled with any of the tan.

The rich tan head fall is truly spectacular.

COLOR ON BODY
The blue extends over the body from back of neck to root of tail. Hair on tail is a darker blue, especially at end of tail.

HEADFALL
A rich golden tan, deeper in color at sides of head, at ear roots and on the muzzle, with ears a deep rich tan. Tan color should not extend down back of neck.

CHEST AND LEGS
A bright, rich tan, not extending above the elbow on the forelegs nor above the stifle on the hind legs.

Beauty is in the eye of the beholder and no more so than when you get this beautiful coated breed in its full glory. A dark steel blue is asked for on the body, with rich, golden tan framing it. In the blue, there should be no signs of tan (this is often what the judges are looking for with the brush). The coat should be straight with a shine.

At a show, you will often see a hubbub of brushes and combs among exhibitors as they strive to reach new levels of presentation in their dogs. However, Kennel Club rules do not allow us to 'enhance' the coat in any way, but we are allowed to use water to help prepare the coat for showing. A show dog will take the best part of two years to grow a full coat. During this time, he will have experienced many hours on the grooming table to achieve the desired result. This is where temperament comes into play. A Yorkie that makes it this far needs to be even-tempered, trustworthy, patient and happy. It is a waste of time to try to show an unhappy dog in the ring. Please remember that not all dogs like this particular lifestyle and it is not worth the stress to you or the dog if it is not to be. If necessary, learn from this experience and move on to another dog.

Exhibitors work tirelessly on the coat so that it looks at its very best for the judge.

SIZE

KC
Weight up to 3.2 kg (7lbs).

AKC
Must not exceed seven pounds.

Dogs seen in the ring would be called oversized by a lot of people. However, judging the size of a dog from outside the ring is extremely difficult. It is only when you put your hands on a dog that you can feel the bone mass and density of what is under the coat. Also remember larger dogs are not always heavier than 7lb; this all depends on how heavy the bonemass is on each dog. Smaller ones can be quite solid, too.

All Yorkies have been bred down from a mixture of dogs that were at least twice the size as they are now in the show ring. The KC rules allow dogs up to 7 lb in weight to be shown, but this does not mean that some exhibitors are not tempted to show above this size. Most of what you see in the show ring is the cream of the crop but it takes a very strong and dedicated breeder not to be tempted to push the boundaries when every thing else fits the Breed Standard. A larger Yorkie can look very good in a big show ring; its longer legs can move through grass and around with ease whereas a smaller dog can look

lost in such a space. Personally, I prefer a dog with medium bone that weighs about 6-7 lbs and no more.

At this point it is up to the judge to feel confident that his opinion fits the Breed Standard. Some judges will forgive a bigger bitch, knowing full well that she will make an excellent brood bitch, which is certainly an important consideration.

FAULTS

KC
Any departure from foregoing points should be considered a fault and the seriousness with which the fault should be regarded should be in exact proportion to its degree and its effect upon the health and welfare of the dog. Note: Male animals should have two apparently normal testicles fully descended into the scrotum.

AKC
Any solid colour or combination of colours other than blue and tan as described above. Any white markings other than a small white spot on the forechest that does not exceed 1 inch at its longest dimension.

When judging dogs, it is essential to bear in mind that this is not science, this is genetics that we are dealing with. Sometimes putting this into

Good sportsmanship is essential in the show world. After all, you know you will always take the best dog home.

practice means that your cuitest and prettiest is not always your best show dog. Keep the following priorities in mind: a Yorkshire Terrier must be balanced in shape, head and body. It must not be too long or short in leg, nor long or short in body. It must have a level topline and a good tailset, it must move soundly and, most of all, have a good textured coat

SUMMING UP

The interpretation that I have given is made from years of showing, breeding and attending seminars on Yorkshire Terriers and other Toy dogs. Reading one book does not make anyone an expert; only time and experience will get you there. Take every opportunity to learn about the breed, attending seminars,

researching pedigrees and breed history, and watching DVDs, so you can find out about showing, judging, caring for the coat, and how to present yourself and your dog at shows.

Remember, breeding and showing Yorkshire Terriers is a journey that can take years, and you will experience both heartache and joy. Always learn from this.

HAPPY AND HEALTHY

Chapter 8

The Yorkshire Terrier or Yorkie, is a breed with real character. In my experience, it is as if the Yorkie is a big dog trying to escape from a small body!

They have a good life-span, which can run well into double figures. As well as having many of the terrier traits one would expect, the Yorkie is renowned as a plucky, faithful companion, a willing friend on a non-conditional basis. He will, however, of necessity rely on you for food and shelter, accident prevention and medication. A healthy Yorkie is a happy chap, looking to please and amuse his owner.

The nature of the Yorkie's coat is a major feature of the breed. There is no undercoat, and the coat is not shed. This makes the breed a popular choice for those with an allergy to dog fur, although time still needs to be spent on grooming the naturally long coat.

There are a few genetic conditions that occur in the Yorkie, which will be covered in depth later in the chapter.

VACCINATION

There is much debate over the issue of vaccination at the moment. The timing of the final part of the initial vaccination course for a puppy and the frequency of subsequent booster vaccinations are both under scrutiny. An evaluation of the relative risk for each disease plays a part, depending on the local situation.

Many owners think that the actual vaccination is the protection, so that their puppy can go out for walks as soon as he or she has had the final part of the puppy vaccination course. This is not the case. The rationale behind vaccination is to stimulate the immune system into producing protective antibodies, which will be triggered if the patient is subsequently exposed to that particular disease. This means that a further one or two weeks will have to pass before an effective level of protection will have developed.

Vaccines against viruses stimulate longer-lasting protection than those against bacteria, whose effect may only persist for a matter of months in some cases. There is also the possibility of an individual failing to mount a full immune response to a vaccination: although the vaccine schedule may have been followed as recommended, that particular dog remains vulnerable.

A dog's level of protection against rabies, as demonstrated by the antibody titre in a blood sample, is routinely tested in the UK in order to fulfil the

The vet will give your Yorkie a check-up when he comes for his booster.

knowledge and advice.

The American Animal Hospital Association laid down guidance at the end of 2006 for the vaccination of dogs in North America. Core diseases were defined as distemper, adenovirus, parvovirus and rabies. So-called non-core diseases are kennel cough, Lyme disease and leptospirosis. A decision to vaccinate against one or more non-core diseases will be based on an individual's level of risk, determined by lifestyle and where you live in the US.

Do remember, however, that the booster visit to the veterinary surgery is not 'just' for a booster. I am regularly correcting my clients when they announce that they have 'just' brought their pet for a booster. Instead, this appointment is a chance for a full health check and evaluation of how a particular dog is doing. After all, we are all conversant with the adage that a human year is equivalent to seven canine years.

There have been attempts in recent times to re-set the scale for two reasons: small breeds live longer than giant breeds, and dogs are living longer than previously. I have seen dogs of 17 and 18 years of age, but to say a dog is 119 or 126 years old is plainly meaningless. It does emphasise the fact, though, that a dog's health can change dramatically over the course of a single year because dogs age at a far greater rate than humans.

For me as a veterinary surgeon, the booster vaccination visit is a

requirements of the Pet Travel Scheme (PETS). This is not currently required for other individual diseases in order to gauge the need for booster vaccination or to determine the effect of a course of vaccines; instead, your veterinary surgeon will advise a protocol based upon the vaccines available, local disease prevalence, and the lifestyle of you and your dog.

It is worth remembering that maintaining a fully effective level of immune protection against the disease appropriate to your locale is vital: these are serious diseases that may result in the death of your dog, and some may have the potential to be passed on to his human family (so-called zoonotic potential for transmission). This is where you will be grateful for your veterinary surgeon's own challenge: how much can I find of which the owner was unaware, such as rotten teeth or a heart murmur? Even monitoring bodyweight year upon year is of use because bodyweight can creep up, or down, without an owner realising. Being overweight is unhealthy, but it may take an outsider's remark to make an owner realise that there is a problem. Conversely, a drop in bodyweight may be the only pointer to an underlying problem.

The diseases against which dogs are vaccinated include:

ADENOVIRUS

Canine adenovirus 1 (CAV-1) affects the liver (hepatitis) and is seen within affected dogs, while CAV-2 is a cause of kennel cough (see later). Vaccines often include both canine adenoviruses.

DISTEMPER

This disease is sometimes called 'hardpad' from the characteristic changes to the pads of the paws. It has a worldwide distribution, but fortunately vaccination has been very effective at reducing its occurrence. It is caused by a virus and affects the respiratory, gastro-intestinal (gut) and nervous systems, so it causes a wide range of illnesses. Fox and urban stray dog populations are most at risk, and therefore responsible for local outbreaks.

KENNEL COUGH

Also known as infectious tracheobronchitis, Bordetella bronchiseptica is not only a major

Kennel cough is highly contagious, and can be picked up at any events where dogs meet.

cause of kennel cough but also a common secondary infection on top of another cause. Being a bacterium, it is susceptible to treatment with appropriate antibiotics, but the immunity stimulated by the vaccine is therefore short-lived (six to twelve months).

This vaccine is often in a form to be administered down the nostrils in order to stimulate local immunity at the point of entry, so to speak. Do not be alarmed to see your veterinary surgeon using needle and syringe to draw up the vaccine, because the

needle will be replaced with a special plastic introducer, allowing the vaccine to be gently instilled into each nostril. Dog generally resent being held more than the actual intra-nasal vaccine, and I have learnt that covering the patient's eyes helps greatly.

Kennel cough is, however, rather a catch-all term for any cough spreading within a dog population, not just in kennels but also between dogs at a training session or breed show, or even mixing in the park. Many of these infections may not be B.

Puppies get early immunity from their mother, but they need to be vaccinated to acquire full protection.

bronchiseptica but other viruses, for which one can only treat symptomatically. **Parainfluenza** virus is often included in a vaccine programme because it is a common viral cause of kennel cough.

Kennel cough can seem alarming. There is a persistent cough accompanied by the production of white frothy spittle, which can last for a matter of weeks; during this time, the patient is highly infectious to other dogs. I remember when it ran through our five Border Collies – there were white patches of froth on the floor wherever you looked! Other features include sneezing, a runny nose, and eyes sore with conjunctivitis. Fortunately, these infections are generally self-limiting, most dogs

recovering without any long-lasting problems, but an elderly dog may be knocked sideways by it, akin to the effects of a common cold on a frail, elderly person.

LYME DISEASE

This is a bacterial infection transmitted by hard ticks. It is restricted to those specific areas of the US where ticks are found, such as the north-eastern states, some southern states, California and the upper Mississippi region. It does also occur in the UK but at a low level, so vaccination is not routinely offered.

Clinical disease is manifested primarily as limping due to arthritis, but other organs affected include the heart, kidneys and nervous system. It is readily treatable with appropriate

antibiotics, once diagnosed, but the causal bacterium, *Borrelia burgdorferi*, is not cleared from the body totally and will persist.

Prevention requires both vaccination and tick control, especially as there are other diseases transmitted by ticks. Ticks carrying *B. burgdorferi* will transmit it to humans as well, but an infected dog cannot pass it to a human.

PARVOVIRUS (CPV)

Canine parvovirus disease first appeared in the late 1970s, when it was feared that the UK's dog population would be decimated by it because of the lack of immunity in the general canine population. While this was a terrifying possibility at the time, fortunately it did not happen.

LEPTOSPIROSIS

This disease is caused by *Leptospira interogans*, a spiral-shaped bacterium. There are several natural variants or serovars. Each is characteristically found in one or more particular host animal species, which then acts as a reservoir, intermittently shedding leptospires in the urine. Infection can also be picked up at mating, via bite wounds, across the placenta, or through eating the carcases of infected animals, such as rats.

A serovar will cause actual clinical disease in an individual when two conditions are fulfilled: the individual is not the natural host species, and is also not immune to that particular serovar.

Leptospirosis is a zoonotic disease, known as Weil's disease in humans, with implications for all those in contact with an affected dog. It is also commonly called rat jaundice, reflecting the rat's important role as a reservoir. The UK National Rodent Survey 2003 found a wild brown rat population of 60 million, equivalent at the time to one rat per person. Wherever you live in the UK, rats are endemic, which means that there is as much a risk for the Yorkie living with a family in a town as the Yorkie leading a more rural lifestyle.

Signs of illness reflect the organs affected by a particular serovar. In humans, there may be a flu-like illness or a more serious, often life-threatening disorder involving major body organs.

The illness in a susceptible dog may be mild, the dog recovering within two to three weeks without treatment but going on to develop long-term liver or kidney disease. In contrast, peracute illness may result in a rapid deterioration and death following initial malaise and fever. There may also be anorexia, vomiting, diarrhoea, abdominal pain, joint pain, increased thirst and urination rate, jaundice, and ocular changes. Haemorrhage is also a common feature, manifesting as bleeding under the skin, nose-bleeds, and the presence of blood in the urine and faeces.

Treatment requires rigorous intravenous fluid therapy to support the kidneys. Being a bacterial infection, it is possible to treat leptospirosis with specific antibiotics, although a prolonged course of several weeks is needed. Strict hygiene and barrier nursing are required in order to avoid onward transmission of the disease.

Annual vaccination is recommended for leptospirosis because the immunity only lasts for a year, unlike the longer immunity associated with vaccines against viruses. There is, however, little or no cross-protection between Leptospira serovars, so vaccination will result in protection against only those serovars included in the particular vaccine used. Additionally, although vaccination against leptospirosis will prevent active disease if an individual is exposed to a serovar included in the vaccine, it cannot prevent infection of that individual and becoming a carrier in the long-term.

In the UK, vaccines have classically included *L icterohaemorrhagiae* (rat-adapted serovar) and *L canicola* (dog-specific serovar). The latter is of especial significance to us humans, since disease will not be apparent in an infected dog but leptospires will be shed intermittently.

Canine parvovirus had a devastating effect on puppies when it first appeared.

There are two forms of the virus (CPV-1, CPV-2) affecting domesticated dogs. It is highly contagious, picked up via the mouth/nose from infected faeces. The incubation period is about five days. CPV-2 causes two types of illness in puppies born to unvaccinated dams: gastro-enteritis and heart disease, both of which often result in death. Infection of puppies less than three weeks of age with CPV-1 manifests as diarrhoea, vomiting, difficulty breathing, and fading puppy syndrome. CPV-1 can cause abortion and foetal abnormalities in breeding bitches.

Occurrence is mainly low now, thanks to vaccination, although a recent outbreak in my area did claim the lives of several dogs. It is also occasionally seen in the elderly unvaccinated dog.

RABIES

This is another zoonotic disease and there are very strict control measures in place. Vaccines were once available in the UK only on an individual basis for dogs being taken abroad. Pets travelling into the UK had to serve six months' compulsory quarantine so that any pet incubating rabies would be identified before release back into the general population. Under the Pet Travel Scheme, provided certain criteria are met (and I would refer you to the DEFRA website for up-to-date information – www.defra.gov.uk) then dogs can re-enter the UK without being quarantined.

Dogs to be imported into the US have to show that they were vaccinated against rabies at least 30 days previously; otherwise, they have to serve effective internal quarantine for 30 days from the date of vaccination against rabies, in order to ensure they are not incubating rabies. The exception is dogs entering from countries recognised as being rabies-free, in which case it has to be proved that they lived in that country for at least six months beforehand.

PARASITES

A parasite is defined as an organism deriving benefit on a one-way basis from another, the host. It goes without saying that it is not to the parasite's advantage to harm the host to such an extent that the benefit is lost, especially if it results in the death of the host. This means a dog could harbour parasites, internal and/or external, without there being any signs apparent to the owner. Many canine parasites can, however, transfer to humans with variable consequences, so routine preventative treatment is advised against particular parasites.

Just as with vaccination, risk assessment plays a part – for example, there is no need for routine heartworm treatment in the UK (at present), but it is vital in the US and in Mediterranean countries.

ROUNDWORMS (NEMATODES)

These are the spaghetti-like worms that you may have seen passed in faeces or brought up in vomit. Most of the de-worming treatments in use today cause the adult roundworms to disintegrate, thankfully, so that treating puppies in particular is not as unpleasant as it used to be!

Most puppies will have a worm burden, mainly of a particular roundworm species (*Toxocara canis*) that reactivates within the dam's tissues during pregnancy and passes to the foetuses developing in the womb. It is therefore important to treat the dam both during and after pregnancy, as well as the puppies.

Professional advice is to continue worming every one to three months. There are roundworm eggs in the environment and, unless you examine your dog's faeces under a microscope on a very regular basis for the presence of roundworm eggs, you will be unaware of your dog having picked up roundworms, unless he should have such a heavy burden that he passes the adults.

It takes a few weeks from the time that a dog swallows a *Toxocara canis* roundworm egg to himself passing viable eggs (the pre-patent period). These eggs are not immediately infective to other animals, requiring a period of maturation in the environment, which is primarily temperature dependent and therefore shorter in the summer (as little as two weeks) than in the winter. The eggs can survive for more than two years in the environment.

All puppies should be routinely treated for roundworm.

There are de-worming products that are active all the time, which will provide continuous protection when administered as often as directed. Otherwise, treating every month will, in effect, cut in before a dog could theoretically become a source of roundworm eggs to the general population.

It is the risk to human health that is so important: *T. canis* roundworms will migrate within our tissues and cause all manner of problems, not least of which

Preventative worming treatment is required throughout the dog's life.

(but fortunately rarely) is blindness. If a dog has roundworms, the eggs also find their way on to his coat where they can be picked up during stroking. Sensible hygiene is therefore important.

You should always carefully pick up your dog's faeces and dispose of them appropriately, thereby preventing the maturation of any eggs present in the fresh faeces.

TAPEWORMS (CESTODES)

When considering the general dog population, the primary source of the commonest tapeworm species will be fleas, which can carry the eggs. Most multi-wormers will be active against these tapeworms. They are not a threat to human health, but it is unpleasant to see the wriggly rice grain tapeworm segments emerging from your dog's back passage while he is lying in front of the fire, and usually when you have guests round for dinner!

A tapeworm of significance to human health is **Echinococcus granulosus**, found in a few parts of the UK, mainly in Wales. Man is an intermediate host for this tapeworm, along with sheep, cattle and pigs. Accidental ingestion of eggs passed in the faeces of an infected dog is followed by the development of so-called hydatid cysts in major organs, such as the lungs and liver, necessitating surgical removal. Dogs become

infected through eating raw meat containing hydatid cysts. Cooking will kill hydatid cysts, so the general advice is to avoid feeding raw meat and offal in areas of high risk.

There are specific requirements for treatment with praziquantel within 24 to 48 hours of return into the UK under the PETS. This is to prevent the inadvertent introduction of *Echinococcus multilocularis*, a tapeworm carried by foxes on mainland Europe and which is transmissible to humans, causing serious or even fatal liver disease.

HEARTWORM (DIROFILARIA IMMITIS)

Heartworm infection has been diagnosed in dogs all over the world. There are two prerequisites: presence of mosquitoes and a warm, humid climate.

When a female mosquito bites an infected animal, it acquires *D. immitis* in its circulating form, as microfilariae. A warm environmental temperature is needed for these microfilariae to develop into the infective third-stage larvae (L3) within the mosquito, the so-called intermediate host. L3 larvae are then transmitted by the mosquito when it next bites a dog. Therefore, while heartworm infection is found in all the states of the US, it is at differing levels. An occurrence in Alaska, for example, is probably a reflection of a visiting dog having previously picked up the infection elsewhere.

Heartworm infection is not

currently a problem in the UK, except for those dogs contracting it while abroad without suitable preventative treatment. Global warming and its effect on the UK's climate, however, could change that.

It is a potentially life-threatening condition, with dogs of all breeds and ages being susceptible without preventative treatment. The larvae can grow to 14 inches within the right side of the heart, causing primarily signs of heart failure and ultimately liver and kidney damage. It can be treated, but prevention is a better plan. In the US, regular blood tests for the presence of infection are advised, coupled with appropriate preventative measures, so I would advise liaison with your veterinary surgeon.

For dogs travelling to heartworm-endemic areas of the EU, such as the Mediterranean coast, preventative treatment should be started before leaving the UK and maintained during the visit. Again, this is best arranged with your veterinary surgeon.

FLEAS

There are several species of flea, which are not host-specific. A dog can be carrying cat and human fleas as well as dog fleas, but the same flea treatment will kill and/or control them all. It is also accepted that environmental

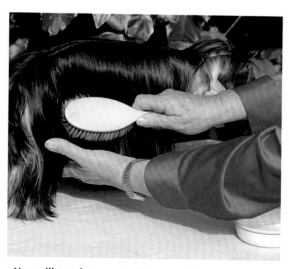

You will need to groom the coat in layers, and get right down to the skin when you are checking for external parasites.

control is a vital part of a flea control programme. This is because the adult flea is only on the animal for as long as it takes to have a blood meal and to breed; the remainder of the life cycle occurs in the house, car, caravan, shed...

There is a vast array of flea control products available, with various routes of administration: collar, powder, spray, 'spot-on', or oral. Flea control needs to be applied to all pets in the house, regardless of whether they leave the house, since fleas can be introduced into the house by other pets and their human owners. It is best to discuss your specific flea control needs with your veterinary surgeon.

MITES

There are five types of mite that can affect dogs.

Demodex canis: This mite is a normal inhabitant of canine hair follicles, passed from the bitch to her pups as they suckle. The development of actual skin disease or demodicosis depends on the individual. It is seen frequently around the time of puberty and after a bitch's first season, associated with hormonal changes. There may, however, be an inherited weakness in an individual's immune system, enabling multiplication of the mite.

The localised form consists of areas of fur loss without itchiness, generally around the face and on the forelimbs, and 90 per cent will recover without treatment. The other 10 per cent develop the juvenile-onset generalised form, of which half will recover spontaneously. The other half may be depressed, go off their food, and show signs of itchiness due to secondary bacterial skin infections.

Treatment is often prolonged over several months and consists of regular bathing with a specific miticidal shampoo, often clipping away fur to improve access to the skin, together with a suitable antibiotic by mouth. There is also now a licensed 'spot-on' preparation available. Progress is monitored by examination of deep skin scrapings for the presence of the mite; the initial diagnosis is based upon abnormally high numbers of the mite, often with live individuals being seen.

Some Yorkies may develop demodicosis for the first time in middle-age (more than about four years of age). This often reflects an underlying immunosuppression by an internal disease, so it is important to identify such a cause and correct it where possible, as well as specifically treating the skin condition.

Sarcoptes scabei: This characteristically causes an intense pruritus or itchiness in the affected Yorkie, causing him to scratch and bite incessantly at himself, leading to marked fur loss and skin trauma. Initially starting on the elbows, ear flaps and hocks, without treatment the skin on the rest of the body can become involved, with thickening and pigmentation of the skin. Secondary bacterial infections are common.

Unlike *Demodex*, this mite lives at the skin surface, and can be hard to find in skin scrapings. It is therefore not unusual to treat a patient for **sarcoptic mange (scabies)** based on the appearance of the problem even with negative skin scraping findings, and especially if there is a history of contact with foxes, which are a frequent source of the scabies mite.

It will spread between dogs and can therefore also be found in situations where large numbers of dogs from different

It is advisable to check your Yorkie thoroughly when he returns from outdoor exercise.

backgrounds are mixing together. It will cause itchiness in humans, although the mite cannot complete its life cycle on us, so treating all affected dogs should be sufficient. Fortunately, there is now a highly effective 'spot-on' treatment for *Sarcoptes scabei*.

Cheyletiella yasguri: This is the fur mite most commonly found on dogs. It is often called 'walking dandruff' because it can be possible to see collections of the small white mite moving about over the skin surface. There is excessive scale and dandruff formation, and mild itchiness. It is transmissible to humans, causing a pruritic rash.

Diagnosis is by microscopic examination of skin scrapings, coat combings and sticky tape impressions from the skin and fur. Treatment is with an appropriate insecticide, as advised by your veterinary surgeon.

Otodectes cynotis: A highly transmissible otitis externa (outer ear infection) results from the presence in the outer ear canal of this ear mite, characterised by exuberant production of dark earwax. The patient will frequently shake his head and rub at the ear(s) affected. The mites can also spread on to the skin adjacent to the opening of the external ear canal, and may transfer elsewhere, such as to the paws.

When using an otoscope to examine the outer ear canal, the heat from the light source will often cause any ear mites present to start moving around. I often offer owners the chance to have a look, because it really is quite an extraordinary sight! It is also possible to identify the mite from ear wax smeared on to a slide and examined under a microscope.

Cats are a common source of ear mites. It is not unusual to find ear mites during the routine examination of puppies and kittens. Treatment options include specific eardrops acting against both the mite and any secondary infections present in the auditory canal, and certain 'spot-on' formulations. It is vital to treat all dogs and cats in the household to prevent recycling the mite between individuals.

(Neo-) *Trombicula autumnalis*:

The free-living harvest mite can cause an intense local irritation on the skin. Its larvae are picked up from undergrowth, so they are characteristically found as a bright orange patch on the web of skin between the digits of the paws. It feeds on skin cells before dropping off to complete its life cycle in the environment.

Its name is a little misleading, because it is not restricted to the autumn nor to harvest-time; I find it on the ear flaps of cats from late June onwards, depending on the prevailing weather. It will also bite humans.

Treatment depends on identifying and avoiding hotspots for picking up harvest mite, if possible. Checking the skin, especially the paws, after exercise and mechanically removing any mites found will reduce the chances of irritation, which can be treated symptomatically. Insecticides can also be applied – be guided by your veterinary surgeon.

TICKS

Ticks have become an increasing problem in recent years throughout Britain. Their physical presence causes irritation, but it is their potential to spread disease that causes concern. A tick will transmit any infection previously contracted while feeding on an animal: for example, *Borrelia burgdorferi*, the causal agent of Lyme disease (see page 130).

The life cycle is curious: each life stage takes a year to develop and move on to the next. Long grass is a major habitat. The vibration of animals moving through the grass will stimulate the larva, nymph or adult to climb up a blade of grass and wave its legs in the air as it 'quests' for a host on which to latch for its next blood meal. Humans are as likely to be hosts, so ramblers and orienteers are advised to cover their legs when going through rough long grass, tucking the ends of their trousers into their socks.

Removing a tick is simple – provided your dog will stay still. The important rule is to twist gently so that the tick is persuaded to let go with its mouthparts. Grasp the body of the tick as near to your dog's

The responsible owner should have a basic knowledge of the conditions which most commonly affect dogs.

skin as possible, either between thumb and fingers or with a specific tick-removing instrument, and then rotate in one direction until the tick comes away. I keep a plastic tick hook in my wallet at all times. There are also highly effective insecticides available.

A-Z OF COMMON AILMENTS

ANAL SACS, IMPACTED

The anal sacs lie on either side of the back passage or anus at approximately four- and eight-o'-clock, if compared with the face of a clock. They fill with a particularly pungent fluid, which is emptied on to the faeces as

they move past the sacs to exit from the anus. Theories abound as to why these sacs should become impacted periodically and seemingly more so in some dogs than others. The irritation of impacted anal sacs is often seen as 'scooting', when the back side is dragged along the ground. Some dogs will gnaw at their back feet or over the rump.

Increasing the fibre content of the diet helps some dogs; in others, there is underlying skin disease. It may be a one-off occurrence for no apparent reason. Sometimes, an infection can become established, requiring antibiotic therapy, which may need to be coupled with flushing out the infected sac

under sedation or general anaesthesia. More rarely, a dog will present with an apparently acute-onset anal sac abscess, which is incredibly painful.

DIARRHOEA

Cause and treatment much as Gastritis (see below).

FOREIGN BODIES

- **Internal:** Items swallowed in haste without checking whether they will be digested can cause problems if they lodge in the stomach or obstruct the intestines, necessitating surgical removal. Acute vomiting is the main indication. Common objects I have seen removed include

EAR INFECTIONS

The dog has a long external ear canal, initially vertical then horizontal, leading to the eardrum, which protects the middle ear. If your Yorkie is shaking his head, then his ears will need to be inspected with an auroscope by a veterinary surgeon in order to identify any cause, and to ensure the eardrum is intact. A sample may be taken from the canal to be examined under the microscope and cultured to identify causal agents before prescribing appropriate ear drops containing antibiotic, anti-fungal agent and/or steroid. Predisposing causes of otitis externa or infection in the

external ear canal include:
Presence of a foreign body, such as a grass awn
Ear mites, which are intensely irritating to the dog and stimulate the production of brown wax, predisposing to infection
Previous infections, causing the canal's lining to thicken, narrowing the canal and reducing ventilation
Swimming – should your Yorkie like swimming, do bear in mind that water trapped in the external ear canal can lead to infection, especially if the water is not clean! Equally, take care when bathing him.

stones from the garden, peach stones, babies' dummies, golf balls, and a lady's bra…

It is possible to diagnose a dog with an intestinal obstruction across a waiting room from a particularly 'tucked-up' stance and pained facial expression. These patients bounce back from surgery dramatically. A previously docile and compliant obstructed patient will return for a post-operative check-up and literally bounce into the consulting room.

- **External:** Grass awns are adept at finding their way into orifices such as a nostril, down an ear, and into the soft skin between two digits (toes), whence they start a one-way journey due to the direction of their whiskers. In particular, I remember a grass awn that migrated from a hindpaw, causing abscesses along the way but not yielding itself up until it erupted through the skin in the groin!

Toys should be checked and discarded when necessary. Major damage can be done if a dog swallows part of a toy and it forms an obstruction.

GASTRITIS

This is usually a simple stomach upset, most commonly in response to dietary indiscretion. Scavenging constitutes a change in the diet as much as an abrupt switch in the food being fed by the owner. There are also some specific infections causing more severe gastritis/enteritis, which will require treatment from a veterinary surgeon (see also

Canine Parvovirus under 'Vaccination' earlier).

Generally, a day without food, followed by a few days of small, frequent meals of a bland diet (such as cooked chicken or fish or an appropriate prescription diet), should allow the stomach to settle. It is vital to ensure the patient is drinking and retaining sufficient to cover losses resulting from the stomach upset in

addition to the normal losses to be expected when healthy. Oral rehydration fluid may not be very appetising for the patient, in which case cooled boiled water should be offered. Fluids should initially be offered in small but frequent amounts to avoid over-drinking, which can result in further vomiting and thereby dehydration and electrolyte imbalances.

It is also important to wean the patient gradually back on to routine food or else another bout of gastritis may occur.

JOINT PROBLEMS

It is not unusual for older Yorkies to be stiff after exercise, particularly in cold weather. Your veterinary surgeon will be able to advise you on ways of helping your dog cope with stiffness, not least of which will be to ensure that he is not overweight. Arthritic joints do not need to be burdened with extra bodyweight!

LUMPS & BUMPS

Regularly handling and stroking your dog will enable the early detection of lumps and bumps, and is particularly important in the Yorkie because of the profuse fur coat. These may be due to infection (abscess), bruising, multiplication of particular cells from within the body, or even an external parasite (tick). If you are worried about any lump you find, have it checked by a veterinary surgeon.

OBESITY

Being overweight does predispose to many other problems, such as **diabetes mellitus, heart disease** and **joint problems**. It is so easily prevented by simply acting as your Yorkie's conscience. Ignore pleading eyes and feed according to your dog's waistline. The body condition is what matters

A well balanced diet and regular exercise will keep your Yorkie fit and healthy.

qualitatively, alongside monitoring that individual's bodyweight as a quantitative measure. The Yorkie should, in my opinion as a health professional, have at least a suggestion of a waist and it should be possible to feel the ribs beneath only a slight layer of fat.

Neutering does not automatically mean that your Yorkie will be overweight. Having an ovario-hysterectomy does slow down the body's rate of working, castration to a lesser extent, but it therefore means that your dog needs less food, a lower energy intake. I recommend cutting back a little on the amount of food fed a few weeks before neutering to accustom your Yorkie to less food.

If she looks a little underweight on the morning of the operation, it will help the veterinary surgeon as well as giving her a little leeway weight-wise afterwards.

It is always harder to lose weight after neutering than before, because of this slowing in the body's inherent metabolic rate.

TEETH PROBLEMS

Eating food starts with the canine teeth gripping and killing prey in the wild, incisor teeth biting off pieces of food, and the molar teeth chewing it. To be able to eat is vital for life, yet the actual health of the teeth is often over-looked: unhealthy teeth can predispose to disease, and not just by reducing the ability to eat. The presence of infection within the mouth can lead to bacteria entering the bloodstream and then filtering out at major organs, with the potential for serious consequences. That is not to forget that simply having dental pain can affect a dog's well-being, as anyone who has had toothache will confirm.

Veterinary dentistry has made huge leaps in recent years, so that it no longer consists of extraction as the treatment of necessity.

Good dental health lies in the hands of the owner, starting from the moment the dog comes into your care. Just as we have taken on responsibility for feeding, so we have acquired the task of maintaining good dental and oral hygiene. In an ideal world, we should brush our dogs' teeth as regularly as our own. The Yorkie puppy who finds having his teeth brushed is a huge game and an excuse to roll over and over on the ground requires loads of patience, twice a day.

There are alternative strategies, ranging from dental chew-sticks to specially formulated foods, but the main thing is to be aware of your dog's mouth. At least train your puppy to permit the full examination of his teeth, which will not only ensure you are checking in his mouth regularly but will also make your veterinary surgeon's job easier when there is a real need for your dog to "Open wide!"

Toy breeds are prone to dental problems, so regular teeth cleaning is essential.

INHERITED DISORDERS

Any individual, dog or human, may have an inherited disorder by virtue of genes acquired from the parents. This is significant not only for the health of that individual but also because of the potential for transmitting the disorder on to that individual's offspring and to subsequent generations, depending on the mode of inheritance.

There are control schemes in place for some inherited disorders. In the US, for example, the Canine Eye Registration Foundation (CERF) was set up by dog breeders concerned about heritable eye disease, and provides a database of dogs who have been examined by diplomates of the American College of Veterinary Ophthalmologists.

A few inherited conditions have been confirmed in the Yorkie. These include:

ENTROPION
This is an inrolling of the eyelids. There are degrees of entropion, ranging from a slight inrolling to the more serious case requiring surgical correction because of the pain and damage to the surface of the eyeball.

HEREDITARY CATARACT
A cataract is a cloudiness of the lens of the eye. This is the hereditary form of the cataract, occurring in the young or middle-aged dog up to about four years of age. It is controlled under Schedule B of the British Veterinary Association/Kennel Club/International Sheepdog Society (BVA/KC/ISDS) Scheme in the UK, Canine Eye Registration Foundation (CERF) in the US.

LEGGE-CALVE-PERTHES DISEASE
Also called Legge-Perthes disease, the problem is more accurately described as an **avascular necrosis of the femoral head**, meaning the ball of the thigh bone dies, resulting in severe

Breeders strive to eliminate inherited diseases from their breeding programmes.

pain and lameness. Surgery can be quite effective. Early diagnosis and treatment through pain relief and resting of the affected back leg in a sling may avoid the need for surgical intervention.

PATELLAR LUXATION

The patella or kneecap is supposed to glide within a groove on the front aspect of the thigh bone (femur) during bending and straightening of the knee joint. The term 'patellar luxation' refers to the situation whereby the kneecap slips out of position, causing the dog to

hop. There are various underlying factors. The problem may be only intermittent, the patella returning to its usual position of its own accord, or a more constant feature, requiring manual manipulation to restore normal joint anatomy and predisposing to arthritis. Corrective surgery can be performed with variable results.

PORTO-SYSTEMIC SHUNT

Reported as having a breed disposition in the US, there is a congenital persistence of a blood vessel from development while

in the uterus, such that the liver is bypassed. This means that toxins usually processed by the liver enter the general circulation and most commonly affect the brain, resulting in the neurological clinical signs manifested. There may also be vomiting and diarrhoea, and problems with the kidneys and bladder. Once diagnosed, surgical correction may be possible if the abnormal blood vessel lies outside the liver. Otherwise, there are medical means for managing the effects of the shunt.

RETINAL DEFECTS

Generalised or late-onset progressive retinal atrophy is controlled under Schedule B of the BVA/KC/ISDS Scheme* in the UK. Retinal dysplasia is controlled by CERF in the US; a simple autosomal recessive mechanism of inheritance is suspected.

TRACHEAL COLLAPSE

Incomplete rings of cartilage help maintain the shape of the windpipe or trachea, providing an easy route for air into and out of the lungs. Dogs affected with tracheal collapse give a characteristic 'honking' cough as the windpipe collapses on itself during respiration. Excitement, eating and drinking, exercise and pulling while being walked on the lead may increase the tendency, as will enlargement of the heart secondary to heart disease. Obesity can also lead to worsening of the condition. There are various ways of managing this condition, varying from simple actions, such as walking your dog on a harness and avoiding obesity, to specific drugs.

COMPLEMENTARY THERAPIES

Just as for human health, I do believe there is a place for alternative therapies, but alongside and complementing orthodox treatment under the supervision of a veterinary surgeon. That is why 'complementary therapies' is a better name.

Because animals do not have a choice, there are measures in

Owners are becoming increasingly aware of the benefits of complementary therapies.

Consult your vet before embarking on a course of therapy.

place to safeguard their wellbeing and welfare. All manipulative treatment must be under the direction of a veterinary surgeon who has examined the patient and diagnosed the condition that she or he feels needs that form of treatment. This covers **physiotherapy, chiropractic, osteopathy and swimming therapy**. For example, dogs with arthritis who cannot exercise as freely as they were accustomed will enjoy the sensation of controlled non-weight-bearing exercise in water, and benefit with improved muscling and overall fitness. All other complementary therapies, such as acupuncture, homoeopathy and aromatherapy, can only be carried out by veterinary surgeons who have been trained in that particular field. **Acupuncture** is mainly used in dogs for pain relief, often to good effect. The needles look more alarming to the owner, but they are very fine and are well tolerated by most canine patients. Speaking personally, superficial needling is not unpleasant and does help with pain relief. **Homoeopathy** has had a mixed press in recent years. It is based on the concept of treating like with like. Additionally, a homoeopathic remedy is said to become more powerful the more it is diluted.

SUMMARY

As the owner of a Yorkie, you are responsible for his care and health. Not only must you make decisions on his behalf, you are also responsible for establishing a lifestyle for him that will ensure he leads a long and happy life. Diet plays an important a part in this, as does exercise.

For the domestic dog, it is only in recent years that the need has been recognised for changing the diet to suit the dog as he grows, matures and then enters his twilight years. So-called life-stage diets try to match the nutritional needs of the dog as he progresses through life.

An adult dog food will suit the Yorkie living a standard family life. There are also foods for those Yorkies tactfully termed as obese-prone, such as those who have been neutered or are less active than others, or simply like their food. Do remember, though, that ultimately you are in control of your Yorkie's diet, unless he is able to profit from scavenging!

On the other hand, prescription diets are of necessity fed under the supervision of a veterinary

With good care and management, your Yorkie should live a long, happy and healthy life.

surgeon because each is formulated to meet the very specific needs of particular health conditions. Should a prescription diet be fed to a healthy dog, or to a dog with a different illness, there could be adverse effects.

It is important to remember that your Yorkie has no choice. As his owner, you are responsible for any decision made, so it must be as informed a decision as possible. Always speak to your veterinary surgeon if you have any worries about your Yorkie. He is not just a dog, because from the moment you brought him home, he became a member of the family.

THE CONTRIBUTORS

THE EDITOR:
BRENDA PIPES
(BREVORDA)
Brenda was born in York, so it seems inevitable that she should own Yorkshire Terriers. By profession Brenda is a qualified midwife and nurse.

Brenda's first Yorkshire Terrier, Penny, joined the family as a puppy in 1977, eventually becoming a brood bitch producing beautiful puppies, including Muffin - Brenda's first show Yorkie.

Brenda has been involved in showing since 1984, becoming a judge in 1988. She has also served on the Committee of the local Canine Society, undertaking stewarding duties at shows and training ringcraft.

Currently, Brenda holds the position of Honoroury Secretary of the Lincoln and Humberside Yorkshire Terrier Club, as well as judging as a Yorkshire Terrier Breed Specialist, and also continuing to show and breed her much-loved Yorkies.
See Chapter Three: A Yorkie For Your Lifestyle; Chapter Four: The New Arrival.

JANET REDHEAD
(JANKERI)
Janet was first introduced to the dog world when she was 12 years old helping a Poodle breeder after school and at weekends. It was there she learnt the art of trimming and preparing for the show ring. She later went on to run a very successful grooming parlour for 25 years.

She bought her first Yorkie in 1958 and has bred and loved the breed ever since. Janet has owned the Jankeri affix since 1964, which is a combination of Janet's name and that of her daughter, Keri.

Janet has been successfully showing Yorkies since 1985, making several champions at home and abroad. In recent years she has become a Championship show judge for the breed.
See Chapter Two: The First Yorkshire Terriers; Chapter Five: The Best Of Care.

JENNY LANGHORN
(LANGHORN)
Jenny was born in Kenilworth, Warwickshire, where she spent the first 30 years of her life. During this time she met and married a local man, Harold, and had two sons. When her first child was quite young, Janet and her family acquired their first Yorkshire Terrier, Scoobie Doo, which started a life-long interest in the breed.

Within five years, Janet had invested in a brood bitch and began to learn about breeding Yorkies from Wendy White Thomas (Wensytes), her mentor and now life-long friend.

Janet and her family moved to Thirsk, North Yorkshire, where her breeding and show career is now based. She has been an exhibitor for 20 years and during this time she has campaigned and made up four home-bred Champions.

She is a Championship show judge and the breed correspondent for Dog World, as well as being a committee member, acting Chairman and Health Co-ordinator for the Northern Counties Yorkshire Terrier Club.
See Chapter One: Getting To Know Yorkshire Terriers; Chapter Seven: The Perfect Yorkshire Terrier.

JULIA BARNES
Julia has owned and trained a number of different dog breeds, and has also worked as a puppy socialiser for Dogs for the Disabled. A former journalist, she has written many books, including several on dog training and behaviour. Julia is indebted to Wendy Thomas (Wenwytes) for her specialist knowledge about Yorkies.
See Chapter Six: Training and Socialisation.

ALISON LOGAN MA VetMB MRCVS
Alison qualified as a veterinary surgeon from Cambridge University in 1989, having been brought up surrounded by all manner of animals and birds in the north Essex countryside. She has been in practice in her home town ever since, living with her husband, two children and Labrador Retriever Pippin.

She contributes on a regular basis to *Veterinary Times, Veterinary Nurse Times, Dogs Today, Cat World* and *Pet Patter*, the PetPlan newsletter. In 1995, Alison won the Univet Literary Award with an article on Cushing's Disease, and she won it again (as the Vetoquinol Literary Award) in 2002, writing about common conditions in the Shar-Pei.
See Chapter Eight: Happy and Healthy.

USEFUL ADDRESSES

KENNEL & BREED CLUBS

UK
The Kennel Club
1 Clarges Street, London, W1J 8AB
Tel: 0870 606 6750
Fax: 0207 518 1058
Web: www.the-kennel-club.org.uk

To obtain up-to-date contact information for the following breed clubs, please contact the Kennel Club:
- Cheshire & North Wales Yorkshire Terrier Society
- Eastern Counties Yorkshire Terrier Club
- Lincoln & Humberside Yorkshire Terrier Club
- Midland Yorkshire Terrier Club
- Northern Counties Yorkshire Terrier Club
- South Western Yorkshire Terrier Club
- Ulster Yorkshire Terrier Cub
- Yorkshire Terrier Club
- Yorkshire Terrier Club of Scotland
- Yorkshire Terrier Club of South Wales

USA
American Kennel Club (AKC)
5580 Centerview Drive,
Raleigh, NC 27606, USA.
Tel: 919 233 9767
Fax: 919 233 3627
Email: info@akc.org
Web: www.akc.org

United Kennel Club (UKC)
100 E Kilgore Rd, Kalamazoo,
MI 49002-5584, USA.
Tel: 269 343 9020
Fax: 269 343 7037
Web:www.ukcdogs.com/

Yorkshire Terrier Club of America, Inc.
PO Box 6204, Elizabethtown,
KY 427026204, USA.
Web: www.ytca.org

For contact details of regional clubs, please contact the Yorkshire Terrier Club of America.

AUSTRALIA
Australian National Kennel Council (ANKC)
The Australian National Kennel Council is the administrative body for pure breed canine affairs in Australia. It does not, however, deal directly with dog exhibitors, breeders or judges. For information pertaining to breeders, clubs or shows, please contact the relevant State or Territory Controlling Body.

Dogs Australian Capital Teritory
PO Box 815, Dickson ACT 2602
Tel: (02) 6241 4404
Fax: (02) 6241 1129
Email: administrator@dogsact.org.au
Web: www.dogsact.org.au

Dogs New South Wales
PO Box 632, St Marys, NSW 1790
Tel: (02) 9834 3022 or 1300 728 022
(NSW Only)
Fax: (02) 9834 3872
Email: info@dogsnsw.org.au
Web: www.dogsnsw.org.au

Dogs Northern Territory
PO Box 37521, Winnellie NT 0821
Tel: (08) 8984 3570
Fax: (08) 8984 3409
Email: admin@dogsnt.com.au
Web: www.dogsnt.com.au

Dogs Queensland
PO Box 495, Fortitude Valley Qld 4006
Tel: (07) 3252 2661
Fax: (07) 3252 3864
Email: info@dogsqueensland.org.au
Web: www.dogsqueensland.org.au

Dogs South Australia
PO Box 844
Prospect East SA 5082
Tel: (08) 8349 4797
Fax: (08) 8262 5751
Email: info@dogssa.com.au
Web: www.dogssa.com.au

Tasmanian Canine Association Inc
The Rothman Building
PO Box 116
Glenorchy Tas 7010
Tel: (03) 6272 9443
Fax: (03) 6273 0844
Email: tca@iprimus.com.au
Web: www.tasdogs.com

Dogs Victoria
Locked Bag K9
Cranbourne VIC 3977
Tel: (03)9788 2500
Fax: (03) 9788 2599
Email: office@dogsvictoria.org.au
Web: www.dogsvictoria.org.au

Dogs Western Australia
PO Box 1404
Canning Vale WA 6970
Tel: (08) 9455 1188
Fax: (08) 9455 1190
Email: k9@dogswest.com
Web: www.dogswest.com

INTERNATIONAL
Fédération Cynologique Internationalé (FCI)/World Canine Organisation
Place Albert 1er, 13, B-6530 Thuin,
Belgium.
Tel: +32 71 59.12.38
Fax: +32 71 59.22.29
Web: www.fci.be/

TRAINING AND BEHAVIOUR

UK
Association of Pet Dog Trainers
PO Box 17, Kempsford, GL7 4WZ
Telephone: 01285 810811
Email: APDToffice@aol.com
Web: http://www.apdt.co.uk

Association of Pet Behaviour Counsellors
PO BOX 46, Worcester, WR8 9YS
Telephone: 01386 751151
Fax: 01386 750743
Email: info@apbc.org.uk
Web: http://www.apbc.org.uk/

USA
Association of Pet Dog Trainers
101 North Main Street, Suite 610
Greenville, SC 29601, USA.
Tel: 1 800 738 3647
Email: information@apdt.com
Web: www.apdt.com/

American College of Veterinary Behaviorists
College of Veterinary Medicine, 4474 Tamu,
Texas A&M University
College Station, Texas 77843-4474
Web: http://dacvb.org/

American Veterinary Society of Animal Behavior
Web: www.avsabonline.org/

AUSTRALIA
APDT Australia Inc
PO Box 3122, Bankstown Square, NSW 2200, Australia.
Email: secretary@apdt.com.au
Web: www.apdt.com.au

Canine Behaviour
For details of regional behvaiourists, contact the relevant State or Territory Controlling Body.

ACTIVITIES

UK
Agility Club
http://www.agilityclub.co.uk/

British Flyball Association
PO Box 990, Doncaster, DN1 9FY
Telephone: 01628 829623
Email: secretary@flyball.org.uk
Web: http://www.flyball.org.uk/

USA

North American Dog Agility Council
P.O. Box 1206, Colbert,
OK 74733, USA.
Web: www.nadac.com/

North American Flyball Association, Inc.
1333 West Devon Avenue, #512
Chicago, IL 60660
Tel/Fax: 800 318 6312
Email: flyball@flyball.org
Web: www.flyball.org/

AUSTRALIA

Agility Dog Association of Australia
ADAA Secretary, PO Box 2212,
Gailes, QLD 4300, Australia.
Tel: 0423 138 914
Email: admin@adaa.com.au
Web: www.adaa.com.au/

NADAC Australia (North American Dog Agility Council - Australian Division)
12 Wellman Street, Box Hill South, Victoria 3128, Australia.
Email: shirlene@nadacaustralia.com
Web: www.nadacaustralia.com/

Australian Flyball Association
PO Box 4179, Pitt Town, NSW 2756
Tel: 0407 337 939
Email: info@flyball.org.au
Web: www.flyball.org.au/

INTERNATIONAL

World Canine Freestyle Organisation
P.O. Box 350122, Brooklyn, NY 11235-2525, USA
Tel: (718) 332-8336
Fax: (718) 646-2686
Email: wcfodogs@aol.com
Web: www.worldcaninefreestyle.org

HEALTH

UK

Alternative Veterinary Medicine Centre
Chinham House, Stanford in the Vale,
Oxfordshire, SN7 8NQ
Tel: 01367 710324
Fax: 01367 718243
Web: www.alternativevet.org/

British Small Animal Veterinary Association
Woodrow House, 1 Telford Way,
Waterwells Business Park, Quedgeley,
Gloucestershire, GL2 2AB
Tel: 01452 726700
Fax: 01452 726701
Email: customerservices@bsava.com
Web: http://www.bsava.com/

Royal College of Veterinary Surgeons
Belgravia House, 62-64 Horseferry Road,
London, SW1P 2AF
Tel: 0207 222 2001
Fax: 0207 222 2004
Email: admin@rcvs.org.uk
Web: www.rcvs.org.uk

USA

American Holistic Veterinary Medical Association
2218 Old Emmorton Road
Bel Air, MD 21015
Tel: 410 569 0795
Fax 410 569 2346
Email: office@ahvma.org
Web: www.ahvma.org/

American Veterinary Medical Association
1931 North Meacham Road, Suite 100,
Schaumburg, IL 60173-4360, USA.
Tel: 800 248 2862
Fax: 847 925 1329
Web: www.avma.org

American College of Veterinary Surgeons
19785 Crystal Rock Dr, Suite 305
Germantown, MD 20874, USA.
Tel: 301 916 0200
Toll Free: 877 217 2287
Fax: 301 916 2287
Email: acvs@acvs.org
Web: www.acvs.org/

AUSTRALIA

Australian Holistic Vets
Web: www.ahv.com.au/

Australian Small Animal Veterinary Association
40/6 Herbert Street, St Leonards, NSW 2065, Australia.
Tel: 02 9431 5090
Fax: 02 9437 9068
Email: asava@ava.com.au
Web: www.asava.com.au

Australian Veterinary Association
Unit 40, 6 Herbert Street, St Leonards, NSW 2065, Australia.
Tel: 02 9431 5000
Fax: 02 9437 9068
Web: www.ava.com.au

Australian College Veterinary Scientists
Building 3, Garden City Office Park,
2404 Logan Road, Eight Mile Plains,
Queensland 4113, Australia.
Tel: 07 3423 2016
Fax: 07 3423 2977
Email: admin@acvs.org.au
Web: http://acvsc.org.au

ASSISTANCE DOGS

Canine Partners
Mill Lane, Heyshott, Midhurst,
GU29 0ED
Tel: 08456 580480
Fax: 08456 580481
Web: www.caninepartners.co.uk

Dogs for the Disabled
The Frances Hay Centre, Blacklocks Hill,
Banbury, Oxon, OX17 2BS
Tel: 01295 252600
Web: www.dogsforthedisabled.org

Guide Dogs for the Blind Association
Burghfield Common, Reading, RG7 3YG
Tel: 01189 835555
Fax: 01189 835433
Web: www.guidedogs.org.uk/

Hearing Dogs for Deaf People
The Grange, Wycombe Road, Saunderton,
Princes Risborough, Bucks, HP27 9NS
Tel: 01844 348100
Fax: 01844 348101
Web: www.hearingdogs.org.uk

Pets as Therapy
3a Grange Farm Cottages, Wycombe Road,
Saunderton, Princes Risborough,
Bucks, HP27 9NS
Tel: 01845 345445
Fax: 01845 550236
Web: http://www.petsastherapy.org/

Support Dogs
21 Jessops Riverside, Brightside Lane,
Sheffield, S9 2RX
Tel: 01142 617800
Fax: 01142 617555
Email: supportdogs@btconnect.com
Web: www.support-dogs.org.uk

USA

Therapy Dogs International
88 Bartley Road, Flanders, NJ 07836,.
Tel: 973 252 9800
Fax: 973 252 7171
Email: tdi@gti.net
Web: www.tdi-dog.o

Therapy Dogs Inc.
P.O. Box 20227, Cheyenne, WY 82003.
Tel: 307 432 0272.
Fax: 307-638-2079
Web: www.therapydogs.com

Delta Society - Pet Partners
875 124th Ave NE, Suite 101 • Bellevue,
WA 98005 USA.
Email: info@DeltaSociety.org
Web: www.deltasociety.org

Comfort Caring Canines
8135 Lare Street, Philadelphia, PA 19128.
Email: ccc@comfortcaringcanines.org
Web: www.comfortcaringcanines.org/

AUSTRALIA

AWARE Dogs Australia, Inc
PO Box 883, Kuranda, Queensland, 488,
Australia.
Tel: 07 4093 8152
Web: www.awaredogs.org.au/

Delta Society — Therapy Dogs
Web: www.deltasociety.com.au